MEMOS

To

KIDS

LESSONS

On

LIFE

Order this book online at www.trafford.com
or email orders@trafford.com

Most Trafford titles are also available at major online book retailers.

Printed in Victoria, BC, Canada.

ISBN: 978-1-4269-2227-5 (sc)

Library of Congress Control Number: 2009913216

*Our mission is to efficiently provide the world's finest, most comprehensive book publishing
service, enabling every author to experience success. To find out how to publish your book, your
way, and have it available worldwide, visit us online at www.trafford.com*

Trafford rev. 2/02/2010

 www.trafford.com

North America & international
toll-free: 1 888 232 4444 (USA & Canada)
phone: 250 383 6864 ♦ fax: 812 355 4082

To *Shari*
who made it all possible

Forward

Ronald Parton's <u>Memos to Kids</u> is about an man afflicted with two terrible illnesses trying to seek his children's understanding of and forgiveness for things he did as a manic man and drunken father. It is that, but much more it is Ron himself trying to come to understand and accept the illnesses and the life they allow him to live. Manic depressive illness (bipolar affective disorder) and alcohol dependency (alcoholism) do not leave much room for life. The high suicide rates for bipolar people and alcohol dependants say enough. Ron, as severely afflicted a manic-depressive as I've ever encountered decided to live on, to seek meaning out of it all and to help others. In plain terms it is a chronicle of someone trying to find bits of meaning when life is not much fun.

Alcohol abuse is common among bipolar people. Not long ago, drinking was a common self-medication for hearing voices and being far too emotional. It is not a remedy, but anything to change the pain. Anything to provide even a facade of control over the feelings. Ron is asking forgiveness for what he did and said stone drunk and in severe mood swings. He said and did things that afterwards seem not from him, but it was him, in altered states. From the sick person, the scared person the hurting person. What he did, what he said he did and said, but was he in his own right mind? Ron has to tackle the question of free will far away from the safety of academe. He is a man of very high principles of human conduct whose bipolar illness can involuntarily lower him to the level of complete ogre.

I have seen Ron in melancholia, as the kind person he usually is, and as a raving, manic lunatic. I know the depressed person and the manic as the afflicted Ron. His extremes are frightening. It is all Ron, but not really Ron. It is his voice, his body, his mannerisms, but not his values, he asking his children forgiveness for things done when he was not really himself. He wants to take responsibility and assume all of the postures and platitudes of our self-help times, but cannot completely do so because he did not make himself sick. The terrible fact for all is no one made him ill. Nothing he did or did not do led to the bipolar behaviour you shall read about.

Ron's illness existed long before it was diagnosed. He was for years just an annoying kook. In fact the first medical diagnosis made, of paranoid schizophrenia, was wrong and for a decade Ron was medicated and treated for a disorder he did not have while not treated for the one he had. Further, he lives in a small, socially very conservative city where few appreciate the spectrum and severity of mental illnesses. He lives in an environment where many people assume the medieval position that if you have such an illness, you did something, sometime to deserve it. It is archaic, one hopes newer generations and better information would help those who are afflicted. They have, but not much.

What of the children? They endured the drunken holidays and the shame of having a father always intoxicated. They did not grow up to become car thieves, dope fiends or detached evangelical crusaders. In the end they grew up fine. One is afflicted with bipolar disorder, but they all understand the disorder everyone wishes would not exist.

Whether the reader has a mental illness or has ever experienced addiction or has been a parent, here is a true story about illness, addiction and being a caring parent.

Dr. Bill Gibson

For My Dear Children,

I would like you to understand why I am writing to you. A parent, like the children they create, comes into this world through no faults or opportunities of their own. In reproducing themselves through you, their children, parents want to create an image (person) even better than that reflected in their own mirror. So, I tried my best not to create you in my image, but to make you a combination of all the best I wanted and what I thought the world would like as well. My lack of insight and foresight in creating and perceiving the process had lifelong effects on us both – some were good, and some were bad.

First, please know that I wanted to provide everything in my power toward your material and physical well being. I cannot include spiritual to that as well. The difficulties of my task meant going to school for a long time to get a good job. Through my raw boned and scraped knuckle desire to provide for my family the best I could. I struggled beyond my abilities and got a Ph.D. which landed me a job as a professor – as you know. I went beyond my abilities, but did give it the best I could muster.

But the means became the end. I thought being respected and recognized through the role of professor brought importance to you as well as me. Retaining the fable state of well being became the end of life in itself, the purpose for which I directed my efforts. So losing sight of the real purpose, I turned to the antidote, alcohol. It became the elixir for my failure as professor, as well as father.

Second, as your father, I had a whole head full of expectations of what I wanted you to become, athlete of renown, scholar of unquestionable repute, specimens of great beauty and distinction. I had my perfect children packaged from society's finest assembly line and included in all the Who's Who's. Of course, you remember the terms for this distinction, the incessant pressure to "do as good as you can". What this insistent standard always meant was, "do the best you can according to my standards". Such standards, in fact, smacked of perfectionism – again, not in your minds, but mine.

So now that all the water has flowed under the bridge, almost anyway, although I am not dead yet, let me try and tell you of my brand new perfectionism – in the form of acceptance. I may no longer expect you to be perfect human beings. In fact it will only be a plus if you excel in worldly terms. What you have been through as members of our family and what you have been through personally is quite enough for me to say that your dues have been thoroughly and forthrightly paid in whatever part of the world whose doors you may enter; church, body politic, or any of the various country clubs, or social assemblies of any kind.

Thus, as I give you the gift of this legacy, my testament to you in this will and testament, I want you to know how much I love you – just because you are you and not what I expect you to be or do. So I'm here to tell you I love you! **"THANKS FOR BEING YOU – NO MORE, NO LESS'.** I'm proud to be your father.

Love,

Dad

Preface

Starting this book to those I dearly love and want to have them remember me after I have left the earthly plane is a daunting challenge. My task must begin by first identifying those I am writing to. You know who you are my children and my grandchildren. I don't want to give you a bio because we know who we are talking to.

I do want to comment on who you are in a generic sense. None of us know exactly when we come into this world and no one really knows when we are going to exit it. We are born then we die with a whole bunch of stuff happening in between. Although many observers about claim that most of us are like all other people, but I have to take issue with this conclusion. I think every person who has ever existed and will exist is a unique and identifiable person. Although we have similarities to others, the most important point about us is we are unique individuals. It would take much elaboration about the biography of each one of you to demonstrate all the similarities and differences with others.

I am writing to each one of you as you have individualized your earthly experience. Thus as I make observations about lessons on life, they will be personal to you because as you read what I say it will be easily noticed that you are reacting to my observations in a different way than others. In the last few years analysts have described the concept of DNA which distinguishes you from virtually every other person that has been created.

I think that sometime in the future someone will discover DNA of the soul demonstrating your spirit is uniquely your own never and all eternity will it be duplicated in future creation. This is only a hazy notion of mind at present but I am anxious see how this concept becomes defined in the future and how it is actually measured.

So I am writing to you individually and only you and no one else. You might call it our mutual secret and collectively what we know about each other made be called our book of secrets. These are what you live by. You might even want to know them as your own unique secrets or your own rules of life. You may choose to not share any of these secrets with others or you may decide to pass these secrets which will elevate their spiritual condition. The elevation of one's spiritual condition which causes others to grow is the best definition of love I have ever come by.

The more you share these secrets with others will bring about expansion of your own. And at the same time the best way to bring happiness in your life. One of my teachers in the past used the phrase, give a little and take a little. This is a good life rule and it can apply to any number of different applications of life so as we walk this journey together, you and I, let us walk beside each other to find a way together. As I learned once, don't walk behind me, I may not lead; don't walk in front of me, because I may not follow: walk beside me and be my friend

So let's begin our journey together.

My Challenge to you!

To answer a child's questions! This is what memos are for:
Questions **why** follow the question
What. Man continuously changes - His first questions are ones of why.
Why does it grow dark?
Why does it rain?
Why does the engine go?
Why does it hurt me?
Why must I go to bed?

We are All bound in a network of the forces in the example of Scylla and Charybdis

Memos contain learned beliefs transmitted from parents to children. Most of these beliefs are common to all families however the techniques of teaching them very from family to family. A wide range of beliefs is listed in the table of contents by number. To get the most for you to understand each of the active beliefs think about it personally.. Where do you agree or disagree? Amplify your very own beliefs to reveal who you are as an individual. How is your individuation discernibly different from others' beliefs about themselves?

Your responses are evidence of your personal identity, your own reality. As you think so you are. As you believe so you are. As you believe so you will act. You're thinking, believing and acting makes you the individual you present yourself as. They are who you are as an individual and provide the world your identity.

As you read references to the various beliefs; ask yourself is this like me or unlike me. Answers to the evidence of your personal reality collectively you believe such statements of who you are examining each item in the table of contents as a standard for examining the nature of your reality.

Is it: (1) a law of random possibilities where anyone at any time may assert this belief

(2) a law of mutuality when any dyad agree on a belief.

(3) a collective belief - wide diffusion of belief (common sense)

Or

(4) truth - an irrefutable assertion that the belief is true - usually called fact.

One must become personally aware of his own beliefs. What you believe to be true is true in your own experience. The definition given by a famous sociologist Charles Cooley, if an individual finds a situation as true, it is true in its consequences.

With these memos I invite you to have a hearty introduction to your beliefs. Your parents have had a say in the contribution to what and how you think. They have structured your learning experience. ".. defining beliefs that you receive. What is your parent's conception of the nature of reality? In addition to beliefs your concepts of who you are come from your parents. Core beliefs are those about which you build your own life. The greatest part of you has already been established by ages six and seven. It is important to walk among your beliefs to become acquainted with them, trust yourself. Inform your reality directly. You act directly from your beliefs.

So our ideas define who what and may generate our emotions and feelings. There are parameters of individual patterns and ideas-infinite varieties of actions and unlimited resources.

A great cosmic law states that like attracts like. Always keep this in mind in relation to meditation and in your actions; let God be the source of who you are! If you do this nothing can ever go wrong in your experience. Surrender to God and your life will be as full and complete as humanly possible.

TABLE OF CONTENTS

BOOK 2

MORE LESSONS

MORE MUSINGS

AFTER THOUGHTS

ANOTHER IMPORTANT AFTER THOUGHT

Introduction

There is something I need tell you. When about half of my life was over, I started writing notes about subject matter related to my kids. I wanted to get them reproduced and passed along to them. I did not think I could spark enough interest in them to get a publishing company on board so I discontinued making notes. The scattered pile of notes remained in a pile on a desk in my den, a disorganized pile of papers that remained there for several years.

Less than two years ago, my son Jeff, asked me to write some things so his little boy, Ty, so would have something to remember about me. Since I know my grandchildren would only know me from names on Christmas presents when I die. More is needed. The end may be sooner then later so I must take advantage of time left. What could I possibly leave to him and my other grand children? What might it be? Something they might remember and perhaps cherish. They could look back at it and say, "This is grandpa". Material things are quickly used up and vanish. An idea occurred to me. How about a basket of ideas? Ideas never die; they could be looked at from time to time and see any changes. What you see here is my desire to leave a bit of me to my grandchildren and their parents.

My idea was to put together some of the random thoughts relating to my family I have written over the years, some which were used in parenting. These memos are the result. After putting them together into some kind of organization my sorting and sifting is what you see here. Being convinced a publisher would not be interested and in-as- much as I wanted to leave a small legacy, and it could not be with fame or fortune, I decided to publish these ideas myself. I offer my notes as a small token to those I love and have given my life ultimate me.

Surely my little project up to now would be a superficial exposure, only a fraction of a story which would provide credibility for me as a parent or citizen. I have presented myself as parent in the same manner as I have presented myself all of my life, I put myself forward with what I thought would be good image for "public consumption". This would only be a caricature of a normal and respected human being. Hidden behind this allegedly acceptable façade was a strong man, but a straw man, a skeleton of who I really am, or the man I really know as others should know me.

My lack of honesty has gotten the best of me; I must tell those who wish to remember me-my real self- who I actually am. Otherwise at the time I am cremated, along with my corpse, there will be an unopened Pandora's Box, with the real me locked inside. Inside my self created prison which would come out only s a puff of smoke to be blown away with the wind. I feel compelled to introduce part of the real me to those who care, especially my kids and grandchildren. I need to rip off some of the masks I have hidden behind all my life. Otherwise as a parent, wanting to teach lessons on life, I would not be a worthy teacher or parent at all.

My life has been like a prison, and me the prisoner, has never found much happiness in all the years of my existence. Locked up with what has seemed eternity, I have sought antidotes to cover up my misery. When being put under a microscope, I can say at the very apex of my existence "I can relate to this" or "I can relate to that"; another way of expressing this is to say about virtually any experience, I have "been there done that".

Joy in my life has also eluded me. I certainly understand a bit of both pain and pleasure because of the intimacy with my fellow travellers who have taught me as we have trudged the road of destiny. I know and have lived the heights of ecstasy and will die knowing the depths of human misery.

Completing lessons about the beliefs I wanted to teach my children and grandchildren to know, I sent life stories to press without really telling about the real me. But I need to reveal more some real truth, not that fake me I have presented to the world most of the years of my life. I do this with hesitation because I fear, like John Powell has said, if I expose the real me to you, you will not accept me as I am. However I cannot in my heart continue the charade, my children. What you see is what you get! I hope it will pass your scrutiny.

Not revealing some of my secrets, you would remember me as one who has lived in Potempkin's Village. By reading spaces between the lines, I present to you me, a real human being with flesh and blood. Painted differently, one can only speculate as to who I really am. As my story unfolds you will see behind a thousand masks, everything about me should only be accepted through the Grace of God. Much of what I say should be thrown in the junk pile of life mixed up with thousands of tons like that of other rag pickers.

Why do I need to tell you this before writing to you about lessons on life? I must do it because otherwise anything I write about in my lessons will have questionable veracity. I claim to have eminent credentials about teaching lessons on life. As I tell you about what the real me believes, anyone who may suspect that my lessons are far-fetched are right in questioning them. It doesn't seem they could really be true. They might only be considered far out suggestions; I myself might question them if I had not lived them as personal experience. They would only be considered a conglomerate of embellished exaggerations. They only would be spin. If what I write you has possible counsel at all is based on solid experience.

I have experienced the best in life and I have experienced the worst in life. I teach from personal experience. If I don't in a sense it's sort of like being in a coma for many years, being aware of goings on outside but keeping it inside; my life experiences, when exposed would sound like the ravings of a lunatic. I had enough of that over the years.

Then a remarkable thing happened to me; I had an awakening. I don't know exactly when this came about and I don't know how this came about but my eyes opened and my ears opened and I could really understand me and much about me. In the last few months, my life has dramatically shifted. I have changed from someone not giving a damn about living or dying to really wanting to live. I have searched many years for purposeful meaning; not finding, it. I wandered around aimlessly spiritually dead.

The only one thing that prevented me from committing suicide, the path of some of my best friends in recovery groups, was a nagging fear of what might happen when I die. This should not have made any difference because the life I have been living for many years was like living hell. One committing suicide can not take the pain anymore. My personal pain has been just as great as those who took their own life; I have many times thought of it. So I don't fault those making their suicidal choice. However, for some inexplicable reason I had the will to survive, I chose what in A.A. we call the "easier softer way".

After much hard won searching, I discovered the possibility of living the opposite of hell, a bit of heaven. However, I have come to realize that through wilful choice I created my own hell. I don't know when this came, but somewhere along the way I came to a new realization. Sort of reminds me of what John Milton once said, "one can make a hell out of heaven" or "one can make a heaven out of hell". As I write My Memos, you might ask, "What can living in hell help teach lessons about life? My answer comes in reading Memos.

I believe my choices about alcohol, over a forty year stint with mental illness and other life problems were maladies which just did not happen out of the blue; I wilfully chose conditions that were the seedbed making them arise and blossom. No, they would not just go away with a wave of the hand. Mental illness is part of the birthright for those afflicted. This is very important for you to know kids because many of the bad things in life happen because we lose our direction and make poor choices. It's like one lost in the forest not knowing the way out. Hope can only come by crossing paths with another lost soul and search for a way out together.

I cannot honestly blame the shambles of my life on alcoholism, because I chose to drink alcohol and even without it I had many problems. Alcohol only exacerbated them. It was I who made the wretched creature I turned out to be. Most of who I am wasn't because I inherited it in my genes. After many years of living hell, I know it actually was in my jeans, but not those given me by parents. I know after going to Street University; it was dishonest for me to blame unknown or mystical forces for my alcoholism and some other problems. Let's be honest; drinking problems can't really be blamed on a disease excuse; we must take personal responsibility for them. So when I attempt to teach you lessons on life about drinking and other things I do so because I know what I am talking about.

I have spent many years of my life calling myself an alcoholic blaming it on sickness given to me through my creator God the higher power. But this is not the usual higher power that alcoholics use to try and dissuade their own alcoholism. I have attended countless A.A. meetings at which I, like everyone else, always say something like, my name is Ron and I'm an alcoholic. This ritualistic action is usually followed by a litany of stories about bad things which have been part of our lives because of too much drinking. In fact, drinking alcohol any amount or too much isn't because we have a disease, this rationalization doesn't fit the facts.

Indeed, alcohol is not good for a person for a variety of reasons, but to become blameless and using the rationalization it is a disease does not tell it like it really is; it is telling a lie and anyone who says otherwise is living a lie. To be honest after all that agony, after all those years after all of the time of me presenting myself in everyday life as alcoholic, I can honestly say who I am because of learning through personal experience. I have come to know this from experiential experience based on empirical knowledge; I know from living it.

I don't know what you know nor will I ever be able to, but I know what I know and this comes from the school of "hard knocks". I do not waiver in what I believe; it's what I know because it's what I know; it's reputable and comes as close to the truth as anything I have ever come across in my 10 years of working toward my Ph.D. and from the 18 years of teaching to hundreds of students about many varieties of human behaviour. I never take the position; I know something which you don't know. Yes, I have said this many times in my 18 years of teaching and 10 years preparing to teach. I got paid handsomely for saying I knew something more valuable than my students. How wrong I was playing that established game of hide and seek with students. To all of them and to my kids I say, "I'm sorry,   please forgive me for playing that game, that silly little game, of hide and seek called- **I teach-you learn.**

What I have said about some of those choices made about alcohol apply to other problems in my life. Space, time, and memory don't allow me to account for everything, however, some stand head and shoulders over others. Without question, the biggest one, the one having impacted me the most is morality. I have answered the call of a typical manic depressive.   Describing all of this and speaking of details about this life are too embarrassing to reveal. Certainly they would be X-rated.   Let it be sufficient to say, at times I had the morals of an "alley cat".

For many years I believed God did not exist. I came from the relativity school. Now I live in a secure world knowing right from wrong and try to live it; creating more contentment and serenity. As you read Memos perhaps a little of this will encourage you wrestle with some of the big issues. If you do I hope you come out the victor.

I know from personal experience one cannot really teach something unless they have lived it. Otherwise, in a sense, it's sort of like being in a coma for a long time, aware of everything going on outside but keeping a lifetime of experiences inside, not letting anyone know about them.

Compare your notes and your credo to mine and see if you would have done the same or are you that one and only unique individual I speak to you about.

Read and enjoy!

My Dear Children - (from here-on I call kids)

Re: Indiscretions

I am sorry that in a drunken stupor I broke your Halloween Pumpkin. I know it was a beautiful pumpkin and I still see in my mind raising it over my head and smashing it all over the floor. I remember it was too late to buy another pumpkin that Halloween Eve, so I'm sorry I screwed the holiday up for you.

That pumpkin, I hope you know symbolizes my whole life of drinking while you were growing up. I know my goof ups were hard on you, but I hope you understand that they were very hard on me too. When one drinks, much of their mind does not think right, or to say the least in a number of ways judgment is impaired. So there were many faces to the pumpkin, and I broke it more times than I can count. Once when I hit you in the eye, Jeff, and you had to have 11 stitches to sew up the gash. I know your calling me a "son of a bitch" did not warrant my brutal action.

How many times did I threaten to get drunk if I did not get my way? God only knows the inner turmoil of a drunk when they use booze to numb life's problems. It actually is an antidote to dying and puts the soul and spirit in suspended animation. Another analogy is that our mistakes are like being burned alive. We wait tenaciously to be rescued and at some point, realizing it will never happen, takes our last gasp of air and no one can put the pumpkin together again. The pumpkins and all of Halloween are gone forever.

The only way to regain the loss is to not break your own kid's pumpkin, for you will have kids too one day, I hope. If you don't, that's okay too.

Love,

Dad

To Kids,

Re: On Being Invincible – On Defining a Defect of Character

Hard lessons have taught me that I'm not only imperfect, but life has been a journey with tragic potholes to walk around. My life is the potholes, the errors around which I myself must dodge. I am not the potholes; they are merely the errors I make along life's journey.

Large potholes–larger errors–are like sinkholes. The soil underneath erodes away and they slink into the ground. Such is my life; my mistakes destroy my character and personal support. I cannot stand or walk stable. My fallibility monitors and controls my essence, my will or agency. My option is for a new morality – a new directive.

How have I changed from being the omniscient to being the pedestrian? So kids, I am not an invincible father. My trespasses are undoubtedly too numerous for you to remember. I suppose it is even easier for you to remember my grosser crimes. I definitely remember there are some good experiences. Hazard Lake is still in my memory Jeff where we "hiked" back into the wilderness and you caught fish until you were tired. It was you and me in the raft. Then with you Jenni, didn't we find God together one night?

Before you die which will come a long time after I'm gone, make a list of all those things I have done wrong. Go to my grave, a quiet place of your choosing, and after recording all my mistakes, please try to forgive me for my trespasses. I wish to be cremated, so this task can be your choice to do anywhere in the world.

Yes, my children, I have made a million and more mistakes, almost an infinite number. But the greatest of all is not being able to show you that I loved you. These letters are my attempt to tell you this. Perhaps it is BETTER LATE THAN NEVER.

Dear Kids,

Re: About Environment

Your environment might say to you, I am a clean slate. You may have any impact on me that you choose. I will absorb you and you become part of me. You surround me from conception till death. The influence you have on me I record and it becomes part of me. I am the sum total of everything that happens to me and your God given ability to react to these events.

With you, nothing is imprinted upon me. You and I make me what I am. Nobody fully knows you or me. We are one, yet we are separate. As one we must work together. Separately, we must show how we are different.

I cannot be fully known by you. You cannot be fully known by me. It is only guesses that account for me individually. When we come together there are an infinite number of possibilities. Many outcomes are determined by how we relate together.

There is part of me which stand alone. That is my nature. It is independent and free. Yet ultimately it determines the nature of my journey with my earthly companion. It does not determine my feeling – it is my feelings. It does not determine my thinking – it is my thinking. It is my motivator, my why? Now that I have a why, I now ask you to help me find the how. Oh! Environment, you are my controller. Yet my survival demands that I could control you. Resolve the paradox and be free. Living in it puts you in chains for the rest of your life. So I cry, "Help, let me out. Loosen the chains".

How? I try to no avail. The harder I try, the tighter the binds on me. So they are attached. I am immobilized by a lack of power.

You, environment, are one with me and I hope to be one with you. You may use me, abuse me, because I think that I am infinite, but I am not. You are accountable to me and I am accountable to you. We must co-operate.

The Law of Interdependency offers planetary survival. I owe to you, you receive from me. You owe to me; our dubious balance belongs to both, yet either one can tip it off.

Please treat me reverently. Dignify me with your respect and I will do the same to you.

Love,

Dad

Dear Kids,

Re: Wanting You as My Children

I wonder if every child goes through the agony of trying to decide if they were really wanted by their parents. The acid test, in the form of a definitive answer, may never be known; however certain clues may throw some light on the picture.

Your being here is no accident of nature, although children do come from people's ignorance and accident on many occasions. The same cannot be said of you. When can someone really know accidents through the self-report of the victim? A whole realm of events occurs outside or parts from choice participation have in this matter.

Time becomes critical in determining if one event causes another. If either of our children came to us prior to our getting married, or even if Shari and I had not been married, the choice to have you would take on new light. As much as our first born and second born came several years after we were married, what conclusions can be drawn other than there was a reason you weren't conceived earlier. We hesitated because of our intense desire to complete school and get good jobs, so we could provide well for you. These early desires were in fact fulfilled.

I wish you could have received the full benefit of our blessings. Your timing to come into this world, the adoration and pride we had for you as babies, and all those hopes for you being special children are now abated with my more realistic unconditional love for you. As I leave this, my world and your world I want you know to know that I love you. I want you to know that I wanted you as children, or not be what I wanted you to be but what you wanted for yourselves. I have finally grown up enough to realize you are meant to be your own person.
REJOICE AND BE GLAD

Dad

P.S. As for you Julie and Jennifer who entered our family at 11 and 12 years old, it goes without saying that you were chosen and did not come from any other reason than that we loved you and wanted to take care of you, to set aside the vicissitudes of the world and raise you to adulthood.

My Dear Kids,

Re: How to Find a Friend!

To find a friend, you first have to find a likely candidate. Look everywhere, in every niche and corner. Look at the young and old. Look at candidates from the same sex and look at potential friends from the opposite sex. There are over five billion people on this planet of ours. A certain number will be our bro's and the vast majority will remain as a number. Yet they are significant numbers because without the part they play, our world would not be the way it is. Do not be a skeptic; each person plays a necessary part. There can never be a starving to death for a person on one side of the globe, without there being a gluttonous counterpart on the other side.

In the sorting and sifting which ultimately creates the path to friendships, emerginge out of this human pot- pourri of human flesh and character? From them we sort and select those attributes we like in our friends. After careful scrutiny we invest our souls in the cultivation of those moments when friendship is born and later reigns, over a coffee or some mundane event.

Almost limitless reservoirs of characteristics have the potential for being created. I often reflect on which of this array I demand for my own personal intimate inner circle. By this I mean a bit more than what the early sociologist called significant others. Not as intimate as a sound mate or not as effuse as acquaintances, my working friends don't yield to vicissitudes of daily living. Here are those character traits of my friends which I hold dear -

trust–equality–respect–sound dignity–division of labor–mutual need treatment and love.

Ron

To: Kids

Re: Following the North Star

When you swim in this life in a sea of contradictory values, you will either sink or swim. I wonder sometimes if I taught you how to swim? When I was growing up the world called us the flower children. We were seekers of peace–not war–free thinkers, and "copasetic dudes".

We, the baby boomers, although I was a very early one, had our own ideologies, a rootless force of power, and a wide vision we know of as our dream. Now our dreams have come and gone. What many of us leave are the skeletons with hardly any meat left on our bones. Your father, kids, is one of those skeletons. All I have left are shattered dreams, painful memories, and a flicker of hope. Am I in the process of becoming an old man with few dreams?

Why has life passed me by? Or why have I passed life by? My answer is that I lost my direction and the compass to point to the direction I should go. In other words, I lost my values and became the skeleton with no meat on the bones–my wanderlust for peace was left with only a bold attempt to fill the void in my life. It led to a most carefree existence.

A man or father without a value or a value without a man are both transient views of this world. Can a person with a value exist or does valueless predominate?

I will always insist that values are not only important but necessary things to teach children as the lessons of life. Check me out, kids. List your values on a piece of paper and determine if they are any good. Your values are good if they make you love more. The value of love comes out when self feels good about itself or you love another when you make them feel better about themselves. That included you.

May you always value what is important!

Love,

Dad

Dear Jeff,   April 8, 1992.

Re: Our victories

So many times I have written you letters trying to remedy our mutual difficulties. At this time of celebrating your 22nd birthday, I want to write a letter to mention our victories. It has been a long and torturous struggle for us to get where we are today. Of course, we don't have anything near a perfect father--son relationship, but who does? After what we have been through together, the scars of days gone by will probably always show. Nevertheless, it feels so good for us to get along amiable as two adults can.

Of recent years, I have thought the ideal would be to love kids unconditionally, but I must confess I have never been able to do this. My heart has always desired a professional life for you with occupational and economic success. When your mother and I are long gone, we want you to be secure. All the money, security, material well-being or anything else will only be a shadow to how one relates to God and fellow man. It is important to care. I have found that personal growth comes only by sharing with others. I hope you find this out, too.

It is much too late to try and be a moral entrepreneur with you, Jeff. I am glad that some of your own values have stood head and shoulders above others, for example, to get through school rather than have a fancy car. Of course, it would have been nice to have both, but my losing my job early in life and having to live on a pension prevented this. I know you had to fight for your rights for identity and your struggle has not been an easy one, but it is one you should be extremely proud.

Now that the rough teen years are over and you are about ready for post-graduate studies, I do want you to be aware of the full-fledged backing of the family for this.

I mean this in a supportive and financial way. Together we will get you where you want to go. This is an absolute promise. This is part of our dream. We will see it fulfilled, on our part at least. If it had not been for a great business loss years ago, we would be home free.

This lack of supportive help should not stifle you. You must be your own person and only accept what you wish and need.

I hope this birthday can be celebrated with joy. I hope you appreciate life and the gifts which God has given you. He surely has blessed you with distinct talents. May you always thank God for giving you choices for caring out his will to make it possible for you to live the best you can. He surely HAS blessed us by giving you to us a member of our family. May we always thank him by always loving you? I plan on this. Thank you for being my son!

Love,
Dad

Dear Kids,

Re: What Commandments Shalt Thou Follow?

From the times I first told you no, you probably wondered why I said this. I couldn't tell you little tykes any better than I can tell you now. The only thing I can figure out is that we must obey some rules to ensure our common survival. Anything short of this can be considered some sort of nuisance, or it is at most, illegal. Both stem from the same origin.

Are the no's of life really needed? What would we do without them? Which rules are absolutely essential and which can be discarded? Are any violations of these rules more heinous in your eyes than others?

Everyone must have rules to live by. In addition to promoting moral integration, rules provide a necessary link between the individuals and the social order. More than mere moral consensus, the moral order would not in a general sense survive if it were not for the implicit agreement of that entire adherence to these principles is adaptive.

A multi-faceted society make-up of many layers, invites a multiplicity of rules arrived at by an almost equal number of forms promoting their origin. Within the same social unit, a variety of bodies compete for control over their adherents. Some of these are individuals though many of them are groups. Now with all the rules, is there a common ethic for them all?

It is the universal imperative, "DO NOT DO ANYTHING TO HARM YOURSELF, ANOTHER PERSON, and OR THIS NATURAL WORLD WHICH YOU INHABIT."

You can't look to your neighbor, or your minister, or government, or anywhere else for that matter to find out when you harm someone. You cannot glean anticipatory warning that it's about to happen. Whether it's a sin we are about to commit, or an "act accompli", there is only one way to know for sure. What does your soul say?

A twig of conscience reverberates to the very depths of the soul emitting an insatiable craving to be soul-filled.

And so we fill it. With almost anything that is within our reach. Give me a drink! That was a familiar ring for me. Tantalize me with sexual fantasy. All of these should follow the universal imperative. "Do not do anything to harm yourself, anyone, or your environmental world."

Kids! This is the only commandment I give you.

Love,

Dad

Dear Kids,

Re: Living Christmases

The kids undoubtedly get up first. We already opened a few of our presents on Christmas Eve. That's because my family opened them Christmas Eve and Shari's family traditionally waited until Christmas morning. That's okay because Shari always bought enough presents to cover the evening and the morning as well.

In the early years, I lay on the couch with beer in hand. Mom always said, "Who goes first?" I guess it didn't matter an awful lot because Shari always assured everyone that there would be plenty of presents for all.

One definition of parent is that they provide for all the needs of their children—whether this is an earthly or heavenly parent. Shari was certainly a provider when it came to Christmas and groceries on the table. Many Christmases I could have sworn that the pile of presents would be higher than the tree. You wee ones, Jeff and Jennie, certainly could not see over the top of the pile, even being elevated to your tiptoes. So you, indeed, were not wanting.

But, please remember that a present is not a present. It's what behind it that counts. So, however, convoluted your mother was in stacking presents higher than your shoulders, she was in fact trying to say, "Look, I love you this much".

Ours were always Christmas's with a gap. There were hardly ever any of Grandpas, Grandmas, and Uncles, Aunts, cousins or others. We left our homeland, our country of birth, for far away places. Now we give you your own Christmases in whatever land you may choose to live. Give yourself the best present of all "Enjoy your life and be happy".

Love,

Dad
the Pseudo Santa Claus

Dear Kids,

Re: How to Grow Up Right; **as "it is supposed to be"**

According to the textbook, every parent wants their child to grow up to be the best they can be. "Do the best you can", I would always say. While I was saying this, there was always a tiny little voice inside me yelling, "But the best that you can be if it is exactly that which I think you should be". Looking at it another way, deep in my heart was my desire for you to just be yourselves... "According to your dad".

There was no Dr. Spock, no encyclopedia of how to do it, no exposure to t.v. talk shows, no Sesame Streets, it was quite simple. The way it was "supposed to be" was my own creative recipe. There was only one little catch in the recipe. I had all the ingredients there, but I left out the yeast stuff–love. I simply did not know how to arrange all the ingredients to create the right mix so it would bake properly.

Then after I sobered up: I grew up a lot. I started realizing that if you wanted to be a certain product; cake, cookie, or what have you, you would pretty well have to create that product yourselves. Yes, I helped provide the raw material and even set up some forms for you to fend inside of, but ultimately the boundaries were yours, and the timely molding of the product became your task.

So, as I write this letter, I am very unsure of what you will ultimately become, and I'm not terribly worried about it anymore. Oh! If you became druggies or any number of society's misfits– or even like me, the alcoholic–I would be alarmed. My anxieties aren't nearly so troublesome anymore.

I am not okay, but I know you're okay! This is because you are made of the right "stuff". Both of you have the tendency to wear your hearts on your sleeves. One of my deceased friends who committed suicide, once said, "Put your heart on your sleeve and go for it".

So, kids, give it all the gusto you got and go for it. Do the very best you can–not in my eyes–in your very own.

Seeing the sunset after the sun went down

Dear Kids,

Re: How do you greet a Friend?

One has many acquaintances over the years. When you are a frequent attendee of taverns, pubs, lounges, and any variegated place for imbibing or just sheer out-and-out drinking, meeting a lot of different character types is part of the territory. Some of these types just tend to float home naturally without prior warning to other family members, neighbors, or anyone who might suffer the encumbrances of a love affair with booze.

Such was the case in the Parton family. The first stranger brought home was Ron. There were literally hundreds of times Dad went to the bar to calm down after classes and he came home a different person. What happened was indeed a symbolic metamorphous. The before and after was a result of the consumption of alcohol. I became inevitably anxious, and not the fewest of times radically obnoxious.

This new fellow was for all ostensible purposes the bogey man for you kids. This is because you were overtly scared of him; he was whacky and unpredictable. Being afraid to have your friends around when this inimitable stranger showed up – which could likely be any time of the day or night, but most often in the evening.

Then, at other times, a more familiar stranger would appear which included old Bob Dwyer. Others included students, or other preparatory outcasts who wanted lively conversation and booze. Neighbors always are a friendly lot when the booze flows freely. Ours usually came on invitation.

The ultimate group of friends – using this word in a very loose way – was the evening I invited all the riff raff in the bar over to shoot pool for $20 a game after the bar had closed.

Yes, kids, you met many of my friends! I hope most of them are strangers to you now and the stranger who I was has now perhaps become your friend.

Dad

"Trying to please"

Dear Kids,

Re: I Can't Leave Home Without You

The first seven years of our marriage found your mother and I with lots of time for each other. We regularly went out for dinner and on occasion took in a movie. Seven years passed quickly, especially going to school and all. Then you arrived Jenni!

If we had a motorcycle, a special side car would have been built for you. You would have gone wherever we went. When you came along, Jeff, we would have just added another sidecar, so we could take you both. Later on we did get a babysitter once in awhile.

We never learned that when we had you, we were supposed to have time for ourselves - a time of re-commitment and renewal. We were so busy working and raising kids (you) our lives were consumed.

After over a decade of this life purpose, we decided to trek off to Calgary for a weekend on the town. Some things we discovered of our type of parents is, "you may get the parents out of the house, but you never get the kids off your parents mind". Our dinner at Calgary was consumed with kid talk. The evening waned away with kid talk. About midnight or so, we called home to check on the kids by phone. The couple babysitting was gone. We the parents anxious and mad at 3:00 a.m. jumped in the car to check this problem out. We discovered we were the problem, not the baby sitter. Wee hours later we the parents were home checking on the kids. The time was 3:00 a.m. We found you okay, the babysitter was visiting friends. This is one indicator of our over protectiveness.

Since both you had flown out of the nest and later came back in it. The time will soon come when we will mutually set each other free. We know if we love each other we will periodically return. I was told "if you love something set it free; if it returns it is yours. If it doesn't, it never was."

How could it be otherwise than for us to remember the growing pains we have gone through in our family?

It is hard to let loose of something when it has hung around you so tightly. May the strength of that bond sustain you in your moment or hour of need? We are with you at these times and know for sure that because you have endured in our common struggle, you have what is needed for survival. When the lack of survival seems imminent, please remember, "God will never give you more than that which you can endure!"

Don't stay out too late.

Dad

Dear Kids,

Re: Your Connection to Your Parents

Parents evolve as kind of God-like creatures to their children. They emerge with this image very early in life. This image of perfection becomes blurred as the years roll along. In fact, even before the teenage years, children learn that their parents fall somewhat short of perfection.

From birth onward, parents discover that their children are not perfect. We can try to forgive every indiscretion or in the parent's perfectionist ways, can't forgive anything. I was quick to point out your shortcomings and was one of those perfectionist parents who thought the world, including personal habits, etc., should conform to my own judgmental preferences. I don't need to recount here the litany of indiscretions which accompanied you both from the very first time the doctor came out of the delivery room, to now. I suppose that even to the day I die, I will be embellishing my version of your shortcomings and holding you up as legendary heroes that even Dad could not make you into.

I must remember this to forgive is to be forgiven. I forgive you for not being the perfect son and daughter I envisioned in my dreams of fantasy. I forgive you for not becoming the legendary doctor and lawyer whom I felt would have made me such a successful father. I forgive you for coming home when I was drunk all those times and were not the model children you could have been. I forgive you for the many times you didn't bring your friends home for your father would be a raging drunk.

I forgive you for those times I came home and you were hiding in the closet. And humiliated my kids would hide from me in such a way. And when I would find you in my drunken stupor, you hollered "You are nothing but an alcoholic!" I forgive you for hiding! I forgive you for calling me a alcoholic.

Now I wonder if forgiving is to be forgiven. I'll try before I die. You should realize here, however, that some of the sins I accuse you of were my own sins of commission. Is it not true that "What Peter says about Paul says more about Peter than it does about Paul?"

I forgive you,
Dad

Dear Kids,

Re: Let's Go Fishing

One of the highlights of my boyhood years was the thought of going fishing with my dad. I can't remember if we ever did go out that much but my memory is still there.

Every father and son should have something between them. It may be any number of things – flying a kite, hunting for a moose or a bear, going out to a movie together, having a hamburger at A&W, or that which meant so much to me in my dreams, "going fishing".

Instead of having a son to go fishing, my little daughter enjoyed it a lot. We did go a very few times, but as they got a little older, I thought I was too busy with my work and the necessity of drinking. It took a lot of time. In fact, it took so much time I gave up on taking the kids fishing.

I should mention something about some of those fishing trips I remember. A perfectionist is always a perfectionist and it spills over to virtually every area of a person's life. I would expect my children to do everything right on the fishing trips. Consequently I would wind up yelling and swearing at you. Our fishing trips weren't much fun. One of the last trips I remember was indeed a paradox. After stopping at Pincher Creek to get three cases of beer, I felt it more imperative to drink than to fish.

Well! You are no longer kids, but fishing is still the same (although one might not catch as many as 15 years ago). Why don't we go fishing sometime? We might talk about what could have been. We might talk about what our lives were like in the older days. We could relive our trips to Idaho, Disneyland, or let our minds wander. It would be enjoyable. Let's go fishing sometime.

Love,

Dad

Dear Kids:

Re: What Do You Need From Your Family?

Every person requires some needs from their family and other ones are those of the whole family. I have compiled a list of individual and family needs. Look at them closely and ask? "How can I or my family of procreation have these needs met more fully than they were with me and my parents?"

Mutual Needs List and/for Therapy

- We can't live alone.
- Unless we have real communication with other people our life is so dry that we die inside.
- Real communication comes from recognizing their mutual need for each other.
- We need God or power greater than ourselves.
- Meaning comes from concentrating on the powers of living.
- Wholeness comes from physical, emotional, and spiritual.
- "Lifelong process" (we shall lead each other out of darkness).
- We must not judge any other person or his efforts.
- Be guided by higher power.
- We need to love and be loved by human beings.
- Family is first source of satisfying our mutual needs.
- Each family member should have equal rights.
- Each family member needs to have mutual relationships outside the family.
- Families have responsibility and a deep commitment to each other until death.
- Each of us was made as a precious, unique individual, full of the power and glory and majesty that are.
- Being human is imperfect.

Dar Kids,   October 26, 1991

Re: On Giving

You were put on this earth to leave it a fuller and more complete place when you die than what it was when you were born.

Often there is a delicate balance between what the natural order has given you and your obligation to return. Who says? I don't, it just sounds like a good idea to me.

I will just think out loud for a moment. Ron, you grew up on a small farm in Idaho and because your parents wanted you to, because you were not inclined to farm because of being an asthmatic and because of lots of reasons conscious and unconscious buried in yourself and your culture, you chose to get an education. Unfurled from this decision was the most calamitous and at the same time the most joyously inspired experiences that would ever befall a person. It would take separate volumes to account for either side of this coin. It could well be called, The Longest Journey, Parts 1 & 2.

Life has been a dialogue between the dark side and the light side of your being, Ron. You stalemated between these. You are a Ph.D. in Sociology having gone to school ten years for this. You attended a few universities and taught at 5 universities. Now what are you doing with your life?

Unless there is evidence to the contrary, you may be doing more or less what God intended for you at this point in time.

Is it important to get paid for what you do? (That is, make money.) Is it necessary to be acclaimed by one's fellows for what you do? If some of these are not answered yet, what reason is there for being, for living, for helping someone else through a tough time?

All the important battles are not waged for oneself, they are waged inside; they are fought for the purpose of making life a better place for ourselves and our fellows. In other words, when you try to promote your own on others fullness of life, you are giving love. May love abound in your lives, kids! Sometimes you will give with no return to you. At other times you may be given worldly returns most of all - give and give liberally. The world will be a better place for it. At the end of the fight, you can say "I fought a good fight. I left the world a little better place because I was here".

Dad said

"You will indeed reap what you sow!"
I Was Wrong

Dear Kids,

Re: Making Mistakes

What bitter vibes these words bring. Even if I could force myself to admit I was wrong, are you aware of what this confession means? I would have to think that I am in fact less than perfect. I am, in fact, capable of making a mistake. What will people think of me? Better still, what will I think of myself if I really admit to error?

Does making a mistake make me unlovable or more difficult to love? If I am too good to make mistakes, does that make me too good to have a relationship with you? The top side of being perfect is always being right. At 58 (Now 71 at time of reproducing these memos) years old, I am sick and tired of not being able to admit that I not only goof up, but do it on a regular basis. Now when I error, I don't need to blame the other person, call names, or get in a rage. I can recognize I make mistakes, but as important I am able to accept other people for making mistakes too.

So kids! Let it be known to you that I error on a regular basis and I can accept that you do too. I don't need to blame you for my goofs! You don't need to blame me. I don't need to get angry and call names. I needn't think I am inadequate, and you can accept yourself and other people as they are. One of the psychological reasons I drank was to deaden the social world from me, as I could not accept other people. I had a whole repertoire of reasons for not accepting others – which included all the members of my family. A long time in coming, I finally learned the problem was in not accepting me. A self-proclaimed cynic, it took me a long time and much heart rendering sweat to understand what Shakespeare meant when he said "The fault lies not in the stars", it is in us. The me in us lets me know I'm not okay–after all, I'm a manic-depressive and alcoholic–and you are OK if you say you are, or even if you don't say you are. We can be ourselves.

Please remember "I'm sorry, I was wrong", but I don't like to admit it. Thanks for giving me the right to be wrong.

"Learn to forget"
Dad

Dear Kids,

Re: How to Bid a Close Friend Goodbye:

Today we said goodbye to his family and my personal friend - Ted. His untimely death at the age of 53 made me realize without a doubt one must develop a meaning for living. Without it – as we witnessed through Ted slowly fading away – any person will just exist.

I am reminded of what Jean Paul Sarte said when he got to heaven "It's not what I expected". God said, "What did you expect?" Sarte replied, "Nothing". As we become conscious beings, what do we come to expect? To what do we aspire? If we have great expectations and great aspirations we certainly will be disappointed if we do not attain these things.

In our social relationships we continue to have expectations, but the ends are quite different. We might expect wives to be dutiful and caring; children of servitude are expected to be responsible. All these, when gone, can be replaced by other people who, in fact, meet these expectations.

There are some whose part in our lives can never be replaced - those giving us genuine care and love as reflected in their peculiar and unique personhood. Thus, wife is no longer wife but Shari. You are no longer children, rather I know you from the peculiarities of your personalities and when these particulars are gone through death, divorce, desertion, or psychological estrangement, there is something gone. Life has diminished. It's about this. For someone to move across town is one thing, leaving the planet is quite another. That's what this is about.

When a friend dies, a little piece of us vanishes. The closeness, the caring, the love, the sharing all disappear. Even in saying this they are not gone in our hearts. Our cry is to cling to something we lost. Whatever way you cut it, there will be no more fishing trips, no more sitting around the coffee table until any hour of the day or night. When the sun sets, it sets. When life ends, it ends!

So be not afraid to cry, to get mad, capture the moment of death for it is that and only that which brings that cluster of feelings we clumsily mold into an image that lasts as long as we ourselves shall live. Then, in turn, we are encapsulated in the mold of those who count in our world – and it goes on as long as our imagination goes on – for eternity.

My friend is dead today. I must find things to do without him. I must if I am able to survive, find another friend. It's only by doing this that life can go on.

I cried and said goodbye. What door will now open, now that this has closed? After one step is taken, what follows it? The next one! Please help me find the way by showing me what I have tried to show you.

Goodbye, my friend

Dear Kids:

Re: About Imbibing

They are the opposites of love and hate - power or powerlessness. In your daily prayers ask God for love and the power to make good choices after which you can control your life. Remember God is always with you!

Love,

Dad

Dear Kids,

Re: Try and Never be Lonely

When I was growing up I experienced a lot of solitude. The truth of the matter is that I have spent a lot of my life being alone.

As a young person I must have lacked many social skills that would make human contact nurturing. I don't know what all went into my feelings of inadequacy and not fitting in, but I probably didn't have good clothes, I was probably chosen last in selecting teams for softball, and a hundred other little events which, because of my own perceptions, gave me my own license to feel inferior to everyone else.

Being last in line though is okay. Everyone can't be first. In-as-much as I wanted to belong, I fought for attention. My younger years were punctuated by being tougher than the next guy. If I did not outfight them, I tried to outwork others on the job and at school.

These motives resulted in a perfectionist mode as well as extreme competitiveness. These modalities moved me to further isolation in the work world and the need to excel academically. I couldn't trust people; they might impede my advancement.

I now have some belongings in a general sense after I have spent stint in A.A. These are my people now although some anthesis keep me some distance from people.

I, along with most North Americans, consider myself pretty aloof and keep psychologically separate from people. I was alone - and for the most part lonely – from Grade 1 all the way through University. We all ought to join a social group "one the one hand group".

Each of us should have enough close friends you count on one hand. These friends will know all about us and love us anyway. When this happens, we will probably accept them unconditionally, too.

Love yourself as your friends do.

Dad

Dear Kids,

Re: On Forgiving You

Have you ever run across the I'm sorry archetype? Every time there is a guffaw about something, they are around taking the blame for it. On the other hand, there is the self-righteous one. He's the one who's always right – you're wrong, type.

Everyone fits somewhere. As for me, I found you kids were wrong an awful lot when I was projecting my own reality onto you. It wasn't exactly, "what Peter said about Paul says more about Peter than it does about Paul". In fact, what very often happened was, "What Dad said about Jeff said more about Dad than it did about Jeff? Why I mention you, Jeff, is because you received more of the blunt of my wrath than you Jenni.

Ours was a typical family in one sense. While Jeff tended to take to his mother while Jenni was able to relate to me better. Needless to say they both related to their mother better than their alcoholic father. The alcoholic was blamed for a lot of stuff and it was very difficult for him, the perfectionist - to not shoulder the responsibility for much that went wrong.

However, sometimes you kids were wrong in some of the events. When you called me a name Jeff, I think you were wrong. Jenni you were not always the queen of the Nile. It is important to remember that none of us are perfect; we sometimes make serious mistakes which belittle us as individuals.

I do not have an inventory of your indiscretions, unless you were some kind of perfect prodigy there were those occasional times of mild or turbulent disturbance.

Jeff and Jenni, I forgive you with the same compassion you extended to me for my errors. Now these events are behind us, we will create the future which we want. The world is, indeed, at your beck and call.

To forgive is to be forgiven

Your Dad

Dear Kids,

Re: More About Fishing

Let's go fishing and not want to catch any fish.

When you were young, I liked to go fishing. I also liked to drink. The love affair with booze may have been stronger than the desire to fish because some fishing trips were made I'm sure simply as excuses to drink. Later on - of course - drinking was the thing to do on almost any occasion. A real drinker is even known to create drinking occasions even when they don't actually exist.

What about the real fishing trips – those times when we went out in our boat for the purpose of "catching some fish? Well! I'd like you to know in no uncertain terms I expected you to be good fisher persons when I or nobody else showed you how. You were expected to cast the line and reel it in like any expert fisherman. It wasn't a great imposition for me to bait your hooks, although it did interrupt my regular drinking time.

Woe unto you if you got a fish on and didn't land him. If you ever had the drag too tight, didn't reel fast enough, or even said something wrong, I took it upon myself – the great fisherman of all times – to reprimand you severely. You might think the fishing blues were designed for our family. Although I didn't keep your count, on more than one occasion we packed our things in the middle of the night. Never did we blame you for your asthma attacks. They just often came at inopportune times. One of these mid-night departures remains vivid to me. The "first things first" motto was appropriate at that time. While in Watertown, before taking one of you home to the hospital, it was reasons to finish a good size bottle of wine.

What else is remembered dry or rather rare family outings? I remember the good times – both of you catching fish – although I forgot the first one you ever caught. There were moments of warmth sitting around the campfires.

Even our first trip in the trailer goes down as a first. Like sardines, we were cramped into the "old Ford" with you and half the neighborhood kids. Even sitting up in the car all night with a homesick one contributed to this great altruistic feat.

Fun dwindled during adolescence and early adulthood. These outings can easily be numbered on one hand. The grand finale was our Seattle trip, Jeff. It will never be equaled at any time or place, but we even got something out of this experience. We learned to endure and we discovered some values in life which we don't want.

The greatest fish we caught was ourselves. It was the biggest and the best, although we did learn finally that you can go fishing and have fun without counting the first, biggest, or most fish.

Don't catch more than tour limit!

Dad

Dear Kids,

Re: On giving Not to Receive

He who gives to another and expects no return is surely a marvel. He who gives to someone and expects either material reward or recognition surely is a materialistic person. He who gives for the sake of giving and does it out of love will inherit eternal life!

Jeff and Jenni, I hope your journey in life will not be in the search for eternal life, I sincerely do hope it will be like the fulfillment of eternal life. Eternal means the fullness there of not the passage of time. You hold the key to the fullness of life. You can use it to open or close the door of life. It is possible, of course, to place the door partly ajar.

It is clear to me now what is to the good life, I am not going to follow my usual way in telling you how to achieve it but, I want to tell you how the principle of giving has affected me.

I live now not to prepare myself for the next world. I try to be as useful as I can to others. I do all that I can to keep other people in those ways reflecting my God given skills. I have found that God has provided me an opportunity for service. If I don't use them it will be a sin against God and humanity. Your lives will ultimately be measured by how you live, not the actions enacted in the areas of life. Just as a tree is known by its fruits, your lives will be known by the extent which you give. Giving must come from the heart; it is not of the pocketbook.

Let your hearts swell with gratitude and your gratitude touch the lives of those with whom you live and work. Small things like thank you or doing an errand, are the building blocks for the Kingdom. It is not great things we do in life that makes a difference; it is the small things done with love. The cement of the blocks is love. So spread some around, and your lives will be rewarded abundantly, I know – mine has.

Remember - By your fruits shall you be known?

Love, Dad

Dear Kids,

Re: When to Quit Giving

I have told you before that the real reward in life comes through giving. Give! Give! Give! When you are done giving, then give some more. The more you give, we are told, the more you receive.

Despite all the emphasis on giving, I want to warn you of some of the hazards of giving and particularly excessive giving. I should comment on giving what and just how much is too much giving.

We give things which have value. If I give you $100 its value relates to how much I see it means to me and how much it takes from the storehouse of wealth I possess. In fact a gift of $100 from someone may mean more relatively than a gift of $1,000,000 from another. A gift of money has a certain meaning and it has a qualitative value having no meaning beyond its economic base. But what about giving outside the material in the ethereal area.

I can say my spirit groans for the bruised and broken hearted the addict, the spiritually sick, and those suffering from any "meanings of any sickness". The disease of the mind is reprehensible and makes me unable to answer the question, "What's it all about?" Because of the gap in my own life, I have developed an insatiable appetite to reach out to others. There has been a certain amount of success, at least through the awareness of joy in giving. In giving one becomes vulnerable and the risks one takes are stridently hazardous to health. Personal finances are sometimes drained to the limit. Family relations, quality time spent with wife and kids can be minimized. Emotional erosion can only be compared to a raw sore rubbed with sand like abrasive. Spiritual life can become like an abyss where the soul cannot pass back and forth to the body and God's loving hands. This results in a hiatus, producing a feeling of being lost in an ocean storm with no compass, and seeing no landmark in any direction.

Many times I have felt such a loss. Well! The truth is I feel like a person lost in the wilderness. Wandering around I found another lost soul. As a matter of fact, there are a lot of us lost — but we are finding our way out together. We do seem to be going in the right direction. The pace which we are traveling has a great deal of variation.

Now it is important to know that I can help lead someone else out of darkness. Where do you draw the line and come to the point where you must say, I have nothing left; I can't give any more. Here's how I see it now. Don't give more than you can give or have. When do you reach a point where you must say "I don't have any more to give".

That's when you reach a point of mental and emotional exhaustion. I have been there often in my 12 step work (one alcoholic helping another). It's that point where someone other than your family commands more than a night's share of your resources and time. It's the time when others take advantage of your generosity and Good Samaritan effort. It's the time you must recoil or die.

My cup often has runneth over so much it is dry. Be advised; take stock, get your cup refilled or suffer like being in a spiritual wasteland.

Don't workaholic yourself to burnout,

Dad

Dear Kids,

Re: On Being Normal

Re: How are you anyway?

How are you anyway? Let it be known at the outset I never encouraged or wanted you to be normal – unless it was much later in my life when the exigencies of life made me accept my own abnormality. One severely stigmatized can more easily accept the abnormality of others.

My personal struggle with being typed mentally ill was exacerbated by the like fate of my own children. Everyone is abnormal in some ways but that's OK because society condones a certain amount of difference in everyone. But there are certain kinds of differences which are rejected wholesale. One of these, I think is being mentally infirm. Or crazy – if you please! An extensive vocabulary especially sets this abnormality apart as a special case. So what if I am nuts! It doesn't make my kids nuts.

So if you want to be normal join another race besides the human race. You can chew moth balls for all I care; you are still my kids. My only expectation now is for you to be happy – abnormally happy.

What about all the other little quirks that make you different. Jeff, because of my passion to correct your breathing problem I encouraged you to have a painful operation that didn't do any good anyway. I thought you should keep going to that doctor and he would finally heal your breathing problem. Hey Jeff, it's now okay for me to know you have a breathing disorder.

In some ways everyone has characteristics which differ from the average. Some are at the left of the middle and some are to the right. The majority are within the first standard deviation. Classification aside – lest any kind of pigeonholing – I submit whether one is normal or not, depends on how you feel about yourself with such feeling coming from behind the belly button.

If you think you're not okay or alright, then, in all likelihood, you will not be. Feeling okay by your standards may not bring normalcy in the eyes of others.

Recognizing everyone is normal in most respects, abnormal in others, and frantic in still others, why don't we all play the percentages and consider ourselves okay. After all if we are not normal yet feel we are okay, for all practical purpose we are okay. Conversely, if we are normal in thinking we are not okay, we are in a heap of trouble.

So why not accept yourself as you are – normal or not – and everyone will be alright.

I'm not OK and you're not OK

But that is OK!

Dad

Dear Kids,

Re: Please Pick Up After Yourself!

Do children inherit the habits of their parents? Yes and No. They inherit some in like fashion but probably inherit others in variable form. This applies to the physical and may -- with some stretch of the imagination – include alcoholism. The data is not all in yet, but it's socially hazardous to call alcoholism a bad habit.

Perhaps it is not too extreme to think that some of our personal and social ills are inherited too. How many of us can remember our dads saying, "If you had it half as tough as I did you would know what tough is". Or "When I was your age I had it twice as bad as you have it now".

The plethora of social ills is only magnified by our inability to accept differences in others, much less be sure of our own predilections and convictions. We wrestle with those undertakings which promote our own well being weighed against those bringing the best advantage to the collective body.

From the minuscule to the monstrous, leaving your dishes in conspicuous spots infringing on others esthetic or physical space by the overt lack of looking out for your things left in public does two miserable things. It makes me resent your personal idleness. Also creating the very bad feeling in the pit of my stomach that you could be lazy, don't care, or a moment of thinking your inattention reveals a lack of respect for others who must view or walk around your refuse.

All said and done, you have the right to leave your garbage in whatever pile or wherever you choose, but please understand that it is my privilege to say that it is very distasteful to me. So "Please pick up after yourself". I'll try to remember and do the same. When I forget or even procrastinate on a task I am going to do later, please be gentle with me. What I don't do is not an indication of what I know I should do, but that is the tempting trial of my life.

Let's overcome temptations,

Dad

Dear Kids,

Re: Please Call Me Dad!

Why? What's in a name? We have sure names and surnames. We have given names. There's a legion of names we might call festive names. So what's in a name? Well, whatever you want it to be. But I'd like to tell you kids, on those few occasions when I came home inebriated, a little searching found you hiding as deep in the closet as you could get. Your greeting to me was something like, "Get out of here, you're nothing but an " alcoholic".

Of all the names I have been called, that was the worst because I was afraid of the frightening but real possibility of being one of society's great misfits. One of them that might be told he fornicates; this was not a critical issue in itself. What was the issue was the "stigma" which all my family and others impute to such an ignoble pastime as dipsomania.

The name calling goes deeper than this. I have been called one-speck, freckles, red, asshole, S.O.B., F...... Asshole, Fag, Queer and probably a thousand others. Those which have galled me the most, which incidentally I react to with the most vehement emotion, are those which I react to by saying, "If I had ever even one single time called my dad that he would have kicked me out of the house or he would have kicked the royal shit out of me. So kids please call me what I called my dad. Please call me DAD!!

What do you call the other guy - someone else? We are advised that whatever you do (call) the least of these you also do it unto me. Be nice to yourself by not calling your dad anything but Dad. Then you will likely call your friend the right name. Lo and behold you might not even have to call your enemy asshole.

Dear Kids,

Re: MERRY CHRISTMAS, I think!

This is the year ending 1991. Ever since I can remember our Christmases have been screwed up. If not due to my drinking it came from the disappointments or letdowns for great expectations on this of all occasions, joyous. Hardly has it ever been joyous in our family, as you kids well know. Among the various reasons for this I suppose is the unbalanced emphasis on the material. Rather than family closeness our gift exchange determines what members like or don't like.

Intermittent from that fatal morning in 1991, I pause a few days later to reflect on the meaning of Christmas. Now a giant reflection of Christmases of yester-year, New Years has come and gone too. Traveling to Idaho the day after Christmas, spending New Years playing pinochle, looking at family members – those still alive – through the same glasses as years gone by, all coalesce into one big interpretation or smozzle.

I am coming to believe you can take alcohol out of Christmas but you can never take away the alcoholic. They say in A.A. that you can sober up a horse thief and what remains is a sober horse thief. Well on special days like Christmas and New Years old feelings and thoughts well up inside and the seams almost burst as they come screaming out. Even as one remembers an alcoholic like one says, "Maybe I can really get rid of my pills now and be able to lead a normal life". Can I ever face it that the pills are here to stay? Can I also ever face it that I will never lead a normal life?

Tough cookies to eat, I know. Christmas was screwed up and these past few days have been screwed up because I am not normal, that's plain and simple and there's no argument.   Should I apologize for Christmas, then, because I am me and I am actualizing those me conditions and processes?

Yes! There are words and more words! People say "Whatever normal means". Well sitting in my ivory cloistered chair made a comfortable pew for playing head games about the meaning of things like normal. The hard won struggle in the school of hard knocks tells me more about normal. Averages, medians, and other stuff simply don't cut the mustard anymore. Normal is when you feel okay a good portion or a majority of the time. It's playing the percentages with your feelings and character.

Thus, if I had had 8 Christmases since I sobered up and 6 have been clobbered by ill feelings of the obligation to drive to parents on icy roads, nagging resentments of Christmas traditions – take a thousand pictures of kids opening presents – so they can be examined in servitude resenting some well thought out presents which were bought especially for you, and contriving to return them for something better. However, you cut it these kinds of things are not normal.

So do I feel guilty until next year because I am not normal and will be abnormal too? Christmas Bah-Humbug! I may not be normal but you are my kids and I love you whether or not we can afford to buy you a whole bunch of expensive presents. I don't know whether you remember them or not, but when I was drinking heavy so Christmases were literal hell! They may not be normal today, and I am sure not well, but I sure am better and Christmases are better than they used to be, is that progress or not?

Love,

Dear Kids,

Re: Do You Need a Valium?

I want to write to you about what to do when the stresses become too great. Whether one takes drugs, drinks too much booze, gets ulcers or has myriad of personal and psychological ills, some means must be used to reduce stress, tension or anxiety.

I'd like to remind you of some of the tension reducers I have used over the years.

1. A long time ago, one of my aunts told me that if you release the emotions it isn't likely to ever get ulcers. I don't think I took this advice as an ulcer preventative but I have exercised the imperative, unmoral at best, of letting pent up emotions escape vocally. I have yelled my way through life too much. You know this, of course, because you were the brunt of it a good deal of the time. Well! I perhaps should have opted for ulcers or at least a measure of consideration for my family and others.

2. Now one stress reducer which works every time is good old booze. From the time you drink and it gets into your blood stream the tension floats away. It may vary from one drink to many, when you depend on an elixir (booze or drugs) to get rid of the tension. When accumulated you have a "bad habit". When it becomes a necessity, we call it an addiction.

All of these little tension relievers are bogus. They are in fact poisons which detract from good health. Don't take a valium, or anything else. Learn to live with the stresses of every day. Life will be much better for it.

Dear Kids:

Re: Don't Smoke! - It's **Bad** for You

As long as people have smoked, there legions of people will tell you why you shouldn't. Numerous others tend to give it a supportive nod. Another voice may seem like a voice in this wilderness, but it's not it's the voice of your dad. So here's my opinion.

For health sake, "Don't smoke". I didn't start smoking until a young adult. Some perverted notion made me think that a young professor would look more sophisticated smoking a pipe. Needless to say I needed all the bolstering I could get to improve my image.

After several months and years of smoking, the taste of tobacco was quite favored by me. My reaction was to tend my pipe in the neighborhood of fifteen hours a day. I rationalized I never inhaled. I must have thought that, that blue cloud of smoke hovering around my head most of the time would never get into my lungs. Let alone the reality that it saturated everything around me.

Now you kids were obviously asthmatic. Why would anyone be such a fool as to spew forth such raucous poison to the detriment of the health of those you loved the most? To this day the only answer that comes is that I was putting my own concerns over those of my family.

Then, Jenni you tried smoking when you were 12. You were an asthmatic getting her feet wet. Those five days when you were in the intensive care were the most fearsome days of my life. Waiting in the hallway Dr. Metcalf somehow got word that your father was a smoker. His response went something like this, "Anyone who would smoke around an asthmatic person should be hung from a tree by his....." Sparking an intense introspective search some time later, I quit.

So I say, don't smoke. It's obviously bad for your own health and an ecological sense very detrimental to the health of those around you.

Besides, you'll feel better not smoking, it's a lot cheaper, and you don't have to suffer from the dingy filter which accompanies that habit. Also fresh air tastes good. The taste is better when I kiss your mother too.

Dad

Dear Kids,

Re: Wanna drink?

Growing up is a time of testing and experimenting with various living styles and options. Some are of questionable usefulness or valve and others may emit great benefit to the chooser.

A world which is absolutely and irrevocably enmeshed in a word of excitation and stimulation, teasing and fixation with drugs is of special significance, especially for the young.

My kids being like all other kids naturally test the social waters through trial of smoking and drinking. It does my heart good when you asked me to taste booze and often it became apparent it was a bitter and grotesque test. I triumphantly poured the bottle down the sink. Something must have changed your taste later since you periodically go to the pub with your friends.

Smoking is self inflicted which is another matter. It's kind of like life and self inflicted death; one must have a reason to live and a reason to die. Your life battle with asthma gave you a reason not to smoke. Without a reason you just are - the essence of in between birth and death is to live. Yes, drink is the Eden which all people must go through without going around it.

When someone says "Wanna drink?" remember you have a choice. In making that choice I hope you can remember the years of absolute agony that befell our family when I was unable to say no to the invitation. "Wanna drink?" Now the agony is fading into the background, it can only be resurrected through someone I love being unable to say no, just as I was unable to do.

Ecstasy is not on the other side of the mountain. It is not found in the bottomless pit; or in the bitter or sweet wine. It is found in the heart — the eternal storehouse of love. I don't care if you drink, kids, but please, please learn early when to say no (more).

You should not! I've been there

Dad

Dear Kids,

Re: What do You do After You Get Angry?

Kids, without attempting to diagnose the various roots and shades of anger, I want to mention what you have experienced so often – anger happens. There probably is some kind of moral parameter and ethical imperative about the source and target of anger, but having honed the expression of anger in my life to its volatile and tacit level, I offer you little in the way of control.

Yelling at the stars, beating pillows, counting to ten or any number, and a hundred others may be gems in the abstract, but anger happens and its concrete manifestation behaves the grosser patience and tolerance of the most lettered Christian.

Well! For a caring person, that is being concerned about your place in the company of your fellows, the after effects of anger – though not as explosive – are as reverberating in their after effects of anger – though not as explosive – are as reverberating in their after shock effect as the original eruption. The very small and the biggest of issues may be the precipices over which misplaced emotion tumbles. The results are seen in equally minuscule of grandiose ways - from a look of scorn to rational warfare.

Is there any justice through anger? Certainly there is not to the victim. There probably are no victors. Are there repercussions? Yes there are especially to me, your dad. I cannot begin to explain to you in any way that you can understand, but I'll try. I have spent five decades being mad at the world and the inhabitants thereof.

I have been angry at those better than me and singularly to each person less than me. Family and friends were not excluded. Not being the person I wanted to be or thought I should be, left me with a jaded world view. My recourse – take it out on others usually through verbal discourse.

No, my anger was not justified. Nor do I think there is such a thing as justified anger. When I broke pumpkins all over the floor at Halloween or a thousand unrecorded emotional harangues add up to a man dissatisfied with himself and his life.

Yet, between the bad times were lucid tones of good feelings where pride enveloped around you and your mother from knowing there was something good and wholesome. Had it not been for those retreats into a cocoon of security, I would never have been able to work the years I did and I would certainly have had a precarious time of sobering up. Every alcoholic has to have a reason to quit. Thanks kids for being my reason.

Love,

Dear Kids,

Re: On Saying I Love You

I love you kids. I say this unequivocally and forthrightly. Saying it too often may be as harmful as not saying it enough, but not saying it at all or projecting it even in the minutest ways creates an emotional shortfall. Saying it in the wrong way often enough misses the mark that it may well have been left unsaid.

Being guilty of most of these, I'd like to tell you now of some ways I've said I love you and hope that my missing the mark in the past will be reexamined through how I say it now.

Most important, I have loved you by being present in your lives. I know mere coexistence on earth does not love make. When any specimen really cares about the others presence there is a potential for love. Trying to pursue any means to enhance the well being of another is the element of action in bringing about love. Anyone loves another when they try to promote another's spiritual growth.

Here's how I love you. It is self evident when I pray for you to have a good life. Prayer demonstrates faith. I believe and have confidence that you will have a good life, a life which will contain joy rather than sorrow; happiness rather than sadness; meekness rather than pride; humility rather than arrogance; and selflessness rather than self-interest.

Thus, I can tell you from the bottom of my heart that your fulfillment in life is my uppermost concerns. I will always go to absolutely any length which is in my power to promote your well being. This, of course, will not permit me granting you greatness in material means. Greatness, which I wish for you, is the expansion of the heart. May you grow in the expressions of kindness? Tenderness will lead you as you give of yourself to others. Generosity need not be reserved for government tax collectors; it can be used for the most need.

The timeliest of all spiritual laws surely is, "You reap what you sow". We all know first hand what one gives is returned at some place in time, many fold. Don't calculate and weigh your gift, then, let it flow freely from you as a river responds to gravity. When we protect our interests, ourselves, our essence, we are limiting the expansions of creative forces in the universe. Let yourself go as the river, as the wind and see nature as its very best.

Love,

Dad

Dear Kids,

Re: Happy Birthday to You!

There are two kinds of birthdays. One type of birthday is the kind you celebrate when you were born. The other type of birthday is to commemorate other special days like in A.A. beginning a life of sobriety. The latter may be celebrated with a simple feeling of gratitude for being sober, bringing with it clarity of thought, soundness of judgment, and the pursuit of sensible behaviors. When you do any more than this is it is a luxury or anything less is a distraction.

What about real birthdays, those marking that time a creature in your own right? In our family they are those times when the family recognizes the special occasion of your birth. I am tempted to believe there is a direct relationship between the number of presents for you to open and the esteem this family holds toward you. Interesting possibilities arise from this birthday law. At the left side no presents – no celebration of birthday. In the other direction, many presents, much celebration.

Might we per chance conclude if the whole element of buying presents were divorced from the birthday there might be a mere natural display than the giving of gifts of special emphasis would be the amelioration of guilt of not giving enough, what the recipient wished to receive or God forbid giving such a foolish item that it would necessarily have to be returned for a more desirable item.

The permutations and combinations of gift quantities and qualities absolutely stupefy me. What once was a time for a down to earth dinner of interested family members is now superimposed with the necessity of gifts with the ritualistic attractions accompanying them. This includes lights, camera, and decorative candles.

In short kids, celebrate your birthdays and those of your own kids, but give them their due without celebrating the celebration. Celebrate without drinking. This is the resurrection of good celebrations. Whatever someone might give you, receive it with a sense of gratitude. They probably gave it to you for a reason. That's probably because they wanted to. Deny them that privilege and you take away their reason for giving.

Now what do we really celebrate? We do not celebrate the celebrations. We celebrate because it is not the end we actualize, the means may vary – the cause, worth while as it may seem, remains the same. So Jenni and Jeff "Happy Birthday Kids". Have one on me.

Love,

Dad

Dear Kids,

Re: Hey Kids "Get Realistic"

Ours is a world of deception. Made up of five million magicians, each in his own way makes reality into a fantasy and makes fantasies seem real. Most of us steadily walk in those grey areas in between.

Are you to be doomed to a level of boredom and pedantic toil? Are you to be elevated to an archetype in human evolution that eases you from the drudgery of work? What will be your task in life?

Each one's adding begins with the recognition of carnal nature. What follows is a contagious series of transitions linked by moments when time is no longer. Then for reasons which even defy reason, time begins again and we die. It is that period between the beginning of awareness and the end of consciousness as we understand it that my concern as your parent prompts my passion, "What are you going to do when you grow up?"

Soul searching has its own rewards. They come to the soul doing the searching. The most realistic of all sage wisdom is to "just be you". You can't really compare one self to another.

Being realistic is to know who you are and accepting who you are. Expect no more than you are capable. Give no more than you have. Take no more than you need.

You may risk the highest mountain or dive deeply below the sea, your measure as a person is not measured by the height of the mountain range as much as it is the highest peak you have climbed. The depth of your despair matters only as it constitutes a stepping stone to a level of life that emits the Aura that yours is a life well lived, a life spent in doing the best that you can do, a life when finished says, "I have fought the best that I could". This world I give you back my friend, a better place I hope than when I came in. This is absolutely all that should be expected of anyone.
"Be a Winner"

Love,
Dad

Dear Kids,

Re: The Loser

When you were not even born yet, the Russians launched their Sputnik. Its first-ness made them a definite winner in the space race. Now this is not the first time a contest has produced a winner and loser, but it heralded the most famous race of all – who could get to the moon first and subsequently dominate the world scene. This would by idle rhetoric of it were not for everything from the school yard marble game to the silver screen screaming the virtues of the winner standing head and shoulders over the loser. I would like to deal with who is the loser and does he have any importance at all in the world.

I want to focus on the loser because our society places so much attention on the winner. Another reason is because I have been called a loser frequently. Indeed a loser is someone who is not quite up to snuff. If that's all there is to it, I wonder why people get their ire up when they are called a loser. I think it's because the word loser means more than what the word means.

Since I like words to mean what they mean, I'd like to speak on the absolute necessity of a loser. Although life is really no contest, we certainly engage it as though it were one. Our analogous use of game strategy to give meaning to life suggests that winners and losers exist. I still must get back to my point. When I ran track at Idaho State University, if I did not appear to be a clear winner, I would, out of contempt for myself, quit the race. In addition to making me a loser I was much worse a quitter. My version of winning was that you had to win all the time or not go. Now if anyone thinks right five people in a race must come at five different points. It is only one's value that emphasizes one placement over another. Why is this?

The inability to answer that forces me to adopt the notion that it's not winning that counts, but entering the race. It is just as necessary for one to be in second in the race as first, even though few consider it more desirable.

So the essence is not winning its running. The criteria for success is 1) how well did you prepare; 2) what was your ability level; 3) how highly motivated were you; 4) consider the above, did you perform to the best of your ability. That consideration is the mark you will make as a person. "Get to your marks", and "Good Luck".

Be Prepared

Dear Kids,

Re: Start at the Beginning

Some things in life are necessary. Other things are irrelevant or unnecessary. That final lot includes the whole basketful which is not clearly useful or necessary but do have the mandate of being required for a little survival and closer to a must to be part of a meaningful life.

Start at the beginning when you have things that need to be done and easy does it. Let me illustrate with a problem I am dealing with right now. Over a period of time something has been going awry with my car. In-as-much as I am not perfect in this area, I took it to the car man and he informed me it would be one of two things. Both would require removal of the transmission. Being sufficiently convinced the problem was one I would fix. I dug right in. The transmission came out easily and rather quickly for a Sunday afternoon mechanic.

What I soon learned is that the journey is not half way over when you're half way done. New parts in place, laced in proper position (I thought) and many tugs and struggles later. Hours later, more sweet grease, and frustration the transmission would not make that last nudge into its final place. Try everything, more sweat and grease, a few swears and exhaustion. Moral so far – "Easy does it" – take a rest and retrace your steps.

Back to work! Jeff is asked to help for a few minutes. Your snorts, snarls, swears a little bit and thoroughly convinces me that such work – or perhaps any work – is beneath you. My reaction is to be frantic to finish the job. Frantic produces inefficiency and scurrying produces that great flare up between me and you Jeff. My concern is not that you don't know how to put in transmissions or fix tail lights, or emptying the garbage, or mow the lawn or ... My absolute great concern is that you try a task, make an effort to do some jobs that are just no fun. None of us in the family likes to be on the "poop" detail, but someone's got to do it.

So we could not connect to get the transmission lifted into place. After a few more hours, more fatigue, and frustration, I resolve, maybe the spine is not lined up. What an inspiration, maybe to start at the beginning of being half way there. Disassembling everything I started from scratch, retracing each step methodically from square one. Task! Try reassembly again, without anyone else! Inexplicably, with a good bit of nudging, using a pry bar, walking in what I thought was the same footprints as before. This time it went into place. Tomorrow I will snug it up, replace the starter and battery, and with a little faith I'll be on my way. What lessons did I learn from all of this?

Lesson One: Admit a problem and begin to deal with it!

Lesson Two: Do what you are capable of doing!

Lesson Three: Don't ask other people, especially someone you are emotionally involved with to do things you're not sure how to do yourself!

Lesson Four: Do not expect anything from anyone else and whatever comes will be a bonus.

Lesson Five: Know what comes first in your life.

Lesson Six: Be persistent and patient with the task at hand and through perseverance, you will overcome any obstacle or problem.

Lesson Seven: Know your limitations but be willing to take a risk until your limitations become known.

Lesson Eight: Do absolutely everything, covering all options, and let God do the rest.

Dear Kids,

Re: Give a Little – Take a Little

I learned this lesson in a somewhat interesting way. It was when I was taking comprehensive exams for my Ph.D. – in fact a final test to be qualified for this final degree. I had gone to university for some ten years, had undertaken a major research project, completed the language requirements, and finished all those requirements for a Doctor of Philosophy Degree in Sociology. The journey had not been easy. Traveling from a small school in Idaho, graduating 31 out of 39 in the class placed the accomplishment of that as a monumental task. It seemed virtually impossible to accomplish.

The final exam was to be 2 hrs or so in length. All the preparations over, I got prepared for the onerous task. I felt the task was just too big for me. Hence, I sought a power greater than myself – what euphemistically. ??? A.A. people have called a higher power. That power of choice on that revealing moment was to go across the street from the Sociology building and suck down three beer at the Agora house – the home away from home for we graduate students who needed to fortify themselves against the formidable ordeal of graduate school.

Marching confidently toward the exam room, the exam went relatively smoothly. I was waiting for those gut wrenching white knuckle questions. One professor threw me a few curve balls which I swung at rather freely. The exam finished, I was invited out of the room for their deliberations. After what seemed like days, they told me that I had passed.

Feeling that quiet desperation which life can be all about, I approached the curve ball professor and said, "Thanks for making it worthwhile for me, I didn't want it to be too easy". His thoughtful response was, "Give a little, and take a little". I urge you, kids, to treat life in the same manner. There are a lot of times when you gotta eat a lotta "crow". A big bunch! Taking a little is a big part of life. Your success ratio will depend on how good you are at rolling with the punches.

The other is to give a little. What do we give, to whom, and how much do you give. I can't really answer. I give you the following recipe for your use:

Recipe for a full life:
1 full cup of love and forgive.
Mix thoroughly until you can't distinguish one from the other.
Spread liberally over everything you see or touch.

Enjoy the feast,
Dad

Dear Kids,

Re: Make a to Do List Every Day

When I was working and during the ten years or so I went to University, time demands made it imperative for me to not confront tasks from their random appearance in front of me. Rigorous schedules and work demands require a plan of attack.

This plan only works if one is highly motivated, energetic and proven to forget small details of course; it is helpful to have a slate of activities on the agenda. This and the prioritizing of these items is what I would like to itemize.

1. Never choose to do anything in your life that you really don't want to do. With limited time and resources, it is advisable to be selective of the things which we do.

2. Do each thing you do as though it were the second time around.

3. Adopt a union creed! If a job is worth doing, it's worth doing well.

4. Jobs need to be completed! If it is apparent that a job is unattended, no matter how   menial it may seem, jump into it and do it with eagerness and enthusiasm.

5. Give every job the very best you have to offer, however lowly or lofty the task may be. When you err or become tired, give proper attention to your work and your body. Eat when hungry. Compromise when angry. Hang around with others who are like you. Take every hour as though it were your last. Live it with gusto and finish your to do list for today.

Dear Kids,

Re: Philosophy Of Good Living: Develop a Personal Credo

What a task it is to suggest the ingredients of a recipe for a good life. Just as there are many paths which can lead to the top of the mountain, there are many paths for a good life. It is a personal koan to know which one is superior to all others. Is the good life equally multi-faceted? The answer is not easy and the terrain is strewn with pebbles along the way. Sometimes they seem like boulders. Should one walk over them or around them? Take the easier softer way.

I am prepared to argue that the good life is available to all. It is simply the absence of obstacles along the journey. Like darkness is the absence of light, the good life is the absence of those things which bring us joy. Most of these are of our own making and through a long process learning and understanding where things fit, actually their pragmatic and utilitarian value, man is what darkness once was before it was replaced by light. The philosophy of a good life is that process of turning darkness into light or an ostensibly dead person into a live one. Did Jesus model anything else? He helped to make the blind see, or to understand their station in life. To know your place and enjoy life one must lighten up or be awakened to all the possibilities life has to offer and be able to achieve those which warrant attaining the best life possible.

What is the good life?

Life is good when one is joyous, happy, and free. Surely there is more than this. A couple of small but strikingly poignant stance for a life well lived. Their suspicious similarities blend a common meaning behind the words of peace and serenity. These are, I think, are the elements of the kingdom being transplanted from heaven to earth. Heaven only means the place where God resides. The kingdom is the key! Although many spiritual gifts exist, love is the most outstanding of all, because to its sustaining power is the highest ideal attainable.

The good life, then, is to love and be loved. Anyone who has ever loved is aware of what it means. Anyone who hasn't loved will never know. If you love someone, you hold them in the absolutely highest regard. The nurture of that person will be the farthest end. At the end of the journey, when one has fought the good fight, I hope the epitaph will read "Life was a more loving place because he walked here".

Love,

Dad

Dear Kids,

Re: Believe in the God of Your Understanding

When I was a boy of ten years old, I was taught to believe in God. I thought through much later reflection that making a commitment to something such as a belief in an awesome God was a task just a bit too difficult for a tender young mind. Rather than encourage you kids to develop a belief in any God, mine was more an attempt to sabotage any possibility for you to come close to a God of your understanding, until you were 12 and 15 years old when I rediscovered God.

This hiatus has caused me to re-examine some basic and significant questions:

1. Should children learn about God?
2. What kind of God should they learn about?
3. What ways should be used to teach them about God?
4. Should God have a religious or spiritual foundation?
5. Which of his churches should you join, if any?
6. Does participation in one religious organization create a different religious experience than another?
7. How do you determine the utilitarian value of any particular church?

Searching for answers to these questions has opened many paths for me to walk.

Believing that one should not judge another until they have walked a mile in his shoes, I submit that the path to the mountaintop where one likely finds God not only can be found in the face of the mountain but on the sides and back as well. Finding God is like wearing a coat of many colors. Its style may be uniquely yours, but in all weather it may protects another. It feels comfortable and in your estimation it looks good on you. Such ought to be for a God and religion.

Of what merit is to advise you to believe in the God of your understanding? Perceiving God – indeed understanding him in a certain way - does not alter his nature. But our understanding of God in a certain way orders our experience with him and sets the stage for our relationship with him.

Thus, God belief orients us to the world in a certain way. This orientation produces consequences for us. It is these consequences for believing that are my concern. I submit that the advantages for a healthy life, indeed, a full life is greater for believers than non believers.

If this is, what God might you choose to believe in? Anthropoformize him if you wish or let him stand by himself. He is everything the human mind can think of - and more. He is everything you wish him to be. Since it is not possible to show all of God's nature, I will comment on one attribute and suggest this alone to be sufficient reason to practice a belief in him in every day affairs.

God is personal! This implies reciprocal awareness. Awareness with volition invites choices which determine outcomes. This is will, having the power to determine our fate. Thus, God's will work in our lives and our will can work in behalf of God's essence. The intra-link is spirit. Alertness of this spiritual essence creates consciousness. This being the first datum, it must remain undefined.

Levels of consciousness vary from the most simple and low to the highest – that spiritual level approximating most closely man's harmony with God. Unity its call, when man and God are closest.

Thus, you see kids; you may walk any path in life. Choose each path carefully. I hope you choose to walk with God. When you choose God, he automatically has chosen you.

Dear Kids,

Re: Keep a Daily Log

This letter is about keeping a daily log and urges you to recognize the merit of a journal. Different words can describe it. Some call it journal, others refer to a dairy or for still others it is a running record of events on life's journey. I don't think it makes a great deal of difference which method of keeping records is used, however, the following suggestions may have been found by some to be helpful or useful.

A. A personal history, that is your own history, tells not only a lot about you but the events shaping your life.
B. Dialoguing sets the stage for your anticipated interchange with others.
C. Dreams and meditation - how you interpret dreams is subjective and personal; if your perceptions are helpful, combine them with other life experiences to get a broad picture. Meditations are different, they set the pace, provide a setting for experience to unfold.

An analogy I read once suggests that the story line of life and a movie are similar. A movie consists of thousands of individual frames, separately they have an image and mean something, but the meaning of the whole film comes after the last frame is shown. We understand the whole story by adding all the separate meanings together.

A journal is one way of connecting the different components of one's life. Journal keeping has a variety of advantages.

The first one, stemming from my own personal vanity is to simply pass on to my kids or anyone who might be interested some very personal thoughts about life. Not ranked, or any particularly being more important than another, writing in a journal actually helps a person in the conceptualization process. You can think about ideas and develop them more clearly when you discipline yourself to write them down.

Not the least important is that emotional release, reduction of stress brought about by laying our feelings on the table even if it is in the form of pencil and paper. It is an exercise in futility only for those who are not honest in exposing their feelings. If you can't talk about your feelings then, please write them out. Both your life and your personal life will be fuller.

Many things will come as benefits. You will make right in your own mind those "sins" of today which make you less than what God made your potential to be. If you were that a long time ago, you would have never needed to drink.

Finally, remember when you were a child and made marks on the kitchen wall of how much you grew since last time. Well, a journal is that very diary of how much you grow between entries whether they are daily or longer. Write so much or as often as you can. but do write what you feel. One day your life will be an open book and surely it will be your magnum opus.

Love,

Dad

Dear Jeff,

Re: "Son" Will You Help Me for a Few Minutes?

Life, in its many interesting facets, presents everyone with the greatest human gift – the freedom of choice. That is exercised in every act which for all people in all time and places, but within the art of freedom is limits. Every expression of freedom is cast on a background which sets limits, both upper and lower limits, for choice. Never clearly established, these areas add fuel to possibility thinking of what am I capable. Of all possibilities available, what can I do?

Answers to these questions are inextricably ground in the amorphous area of socialization and acculturation. Let me illustrate. When a mere babe, my son told his kindergarten teacher that he helped his dad by getting him a beer out of the refrigerator. Dad must have asked him or told him to fetch a beer.

Over twenty years late, I don't call for a beer. Today when I ask you to help me for a few minutes, make no mistake that I ask you certain tasks without asking your sister. We men have things to do like fixing the cars when they break down, or other man stuff that can be work or pleasure like golfing or fishing. I thought my fatherly task was to teach you to do things right so I thought I should correct your mistakes. Sorry Son, I didn't realize that I did so much correcting. I didn't do enough reassuring or affirming. The inevitable consequence is today when I ask for your help, you inform me we can't work together.

How right you are! How unfortunate for me being a father not to get this kind of nurture from his only son, the kind of nurture that a father – and son too – needs so very much.

Beware son the adage "Like father, like son". What I have described is how I related to my father. I caution you to beware so you don't inherit the same. If you have a son, teach him but not critically, golf together - play tennis, etc.

It may not only save your life, it may also teach you how to be a man. I wish I had learned in time. Like my dad, I played the role the best I knew how, or so I thought anyway. Am I to say that my alcoholism was accidental, by chance, from fortuitous circumstance, or just plain predictability? Alcoholism, is only one strain between father and son (daughter as well). An almost infinite number of others coincides with the strained growth of two structure dissected only by fate or choice and united in eternity by common spirit.

Son, I know you have chosen not to help me, but as I do the job alone my inner voice tells me how nice it would be if we did it together. Thanks anyway. Maybe next time we can work together.

Love,
Dad

Dear Kids,

Re: Let's Take a Holiday!

Kids! Our holiday means that it is special. It's not much different from your vacation. Two words mean the same thing – a time to put away the cares of the world – to get away from it all. While we are doing this, wouldn't it be nice to have some fun, travel a little bit, and as well, have some new or novel experiences.

Your mother and I have planned our lives well. Our education, our children, and our careers all came according to plan except for an original rather small factor which grew to gigantic proportions. We calculated that we would be able to make two "big" trips in our children's growing up years.

One of these came because of fortuitous circumstances a few short years after moving to Canada. Shari, Jenni, Jeff and I made a momentous decision to fly to the Caribbean for a wondrous two week holiday. It turned out to be a wonder alright. It was a two week fiasco or should I properly label it as an extended debauch. Its details should remain buried in the lost rays of sunshine remaining on Tortilla; for nothing important should be resurrected from this experience.

It was so easy, I felt, or at least I rationalized, that since rum and other sundry booze was so cheap, the entitlement to drink was forthright. Whatever the reason, I drank and then drank some more. It was indeed a debauch, prolonged to the length of the two week holiday, Ho blackouts! First comes the teasing paralysis of deranged thinking from drinking. It may have been no accident that my paranoia created a house of monsters as I looked in the books in the townhouse we rented on St. Johns. Replete with suspicious of down, I slithered away into my own cocoon of doom only to be reserved by lucid moments of long suffering hours.

This Caribbean mis-adventure was actually a symbol of my own misplaced fatherhood. Not only did I lose the propriety to this role before my children were born, it escalated as the years evolved. I missed the opportunity to parent, at least in a proper way and certainly the second great trip for our family just seemed to fade out of the realm of possibilities.

Love,

Dad

Dear Kids,

Re: Kids, "I'm a Lover? Not a Fighter".

One thing about the growing up years, things happen which only you kids know about through "war stories" told to them by your classmates during school reunions. Now about those old stories about my fighting business; they were true but only until I reached a certain age.

It started when I was in grade six or seven. Everything that is in a decision to "beat someone up" behooves explanation, however, looking back on it, it was not apparent that I had a deep and growing need to try and demonstrate superiority. The law of the jungle was the same on the short street of New Plymouth, Idaho. Win and conquer was very much my motto. My big brother added fuel to this predatory mentality. He once told me if you fight you should not only get the first strike, but be fierce enough to win. I followed this sage advice until I was about twenty years old.

Unfortunately the battlefield mentality is not far from the kitchen table. There I learned many lessons from your grandfather. He was a dominant and authoritarian soul. So without any pretense, and little forethought, I became like my dad. Social inheritance in fact occurs perhaps as much as biological inheritance.

More important, however, is the psychology of fighting. Winning by conquering is more than a catch phrase. Our society finds it to be real.

Now I am curiously sensitive to harm done to others. Verbal confrontation is just as unconscionable as physical. "Sticks and stones can hurt you, but words can hurt you too". Our cultural heritage parades abuse as much as any cultural artifact. We harbor a collective resentment towards anyone who disagrees with us.

Being one of the over-the-hill gang, I now deplore abuse of any type. War, gang attack, child abuse, a world of conflict must be defused by constant recourse to the source of all peace – love. No wonder the command to love one another is so powerful. Let love prevail in your lives, kids, and peace will surely be yours.

Love,

Dad

Dear Kids,

Re: Drinking Alcohol "Kids, please don't drink when you grow up".

The more I read about alcoholism, the more I think this sage advice should have been given by Victorian parents or early temperance writers. Being dealt a full hand of alcoholic propaganda for ten years, I now tend to swing in the direction from (t - totaler) to a believer in moderation.

The 160 year love affair my church has had in promoting temperance ideology surely must be based in the Washingtonian movement of its time. Why does the popular ideology of the day need to be rubber stamped by the church (section 86) and legions of church going people? You and I should be obliged to feel a burden of guilt tasting or perhaps even indulge from time to time or for that matter, why can't they who serve the sacraments even take as much as a glass of wine?

Jenni, drinking may be different for those of us who must take meds. Harmony and health can't occur if we foul up the medicinal process with alcohol. Other than this I see no reason that we should not do what is socially proper and acceptable.

Of course, propriety must be the rule of the day. I strongly believe if you raise a child up the way he ought to be he will not depart from it. Train a child on the use of alcohol, and in all likelihood he will learn to use it properly.

In contrast is the conflict paradigm. Tell a child drinking is a No! No! One day if they are socially conscious, they will rebel. As is the case often in this mode rebellion, it takes in horrendous proportions.

Say No Thanks; it is unhealthy

Love,

Dad

Dear Kids,

Re: Good Morning - Kids "

Good morning! What kind of day are you going to have? Now this would not be such an important a" Good question were it not for my urge to greet you amiably this morning only to be received by a snarl or growl. Actually the reaction behooves description, but it made me think about some things as I walked out the door without ever trying to emit a goodbye.

Recognizing that in the way we start a day determines a lot how the day will turn out, unusual or irregular; I might even call it insensitive or immature. Greeting a morning, with "I don't feel very good" is not going to ruin my day. It makes me think, however, that how I start my day may have important consequences for myself and others. Given this I leave it for you to fill in. It will be pretty much what you think it will be.

More precisely, you can be about as content as you want to be today. You can be happy, sad, anxious or tense, relaxed or taught. What happens to you and your body today depends on you. May I suggest that it helps to get a good start if you begin with some meditation and thought provoking prayer? There are numerous meditation books available today. Choose your own! It can work miracles. A prayer – even a short "Good Morning Lord" can also work miracles. What can I do for you today, God, can set the tone for the day!

Greeting the day with a frown or smile is the first step of the day. It is kind of like the appetizer for a scrumptious meal; it is a taste of things to come. Minute by minute through the day we reflect on how it started; we also assess how it is going. I will chart this day from time-to-time along the way. I am determined that regardless of how it started, how difficult it was for me to choke out a greeting and be rebuffed, my day is going to be a good one. God knows so many were not.

The awful anxious task of teaching a few hours and spending the rest of the day in the pub is reminder enough of a number of years in days gone by. So today - the only day I know and am able to control is today. I want to make the best of it. I hope you have a good day!

This is the day the Lord has made
"Rejoice in it!"

Dad

Dear Kids,

Re: Be Careful Not to Pick up Strangers

Some bits of advice apply to adults as well as kids. They also apply to the one
giving as much as the intended receiver. I look at myself today, a man of 55-
(now 20 years later since I started writing this). Years older I have not been
paying close attention to my own advice.

Our complex world, not like Henry David Thoreau's "Walden", forces us
to face many monsters, in the supermarket, churches, restaurants etc. Many
times people are in desperate search for contact with another maybe, a smile,
a hello, any number of greetings.

People are desperately hungry. Not so much for food for the body, but
for food for the soul.

Why such desperation hosts in feeding the soul, only the Hungary
knows? When you want, what do you offer the one you meet, and what are
they to you. You can offer yourself, but what manner of person is nurtured by
the skin of my skin and bones of my bones. What moment of sensuous ecstasy
is equivalent to what I am coming to endearingly call a spiritual orgasm?
Crude? Yes! The very intricate quintessence cannot be equaled by any physical
doing.

So says with me and me with you, if you are a dear stranger. The two
of us meet on the high road of the journey, not the low road of graveling
sexuality. What will I do with your bent spirit? Well, our sojourn is so great,
me a lonely unfilled man; you whatever you say you are. What do you need
dear stranger?

What can two people do that doesn't violate the personal code of either,
or the code of universal truth; a moral compass to enjoy? Indeed, titillation
of the body gives rapture to the

Spirit. Is the spirit touched by talk of fancy minor things, politics,
religion, or any sundry things which flutter by consciousness? Is there a
yearning for deeper things of the heart?

"Stranger", I say, "Who are you anyway?" Does it suffice me to know
your age, religion, and status of marriage? One of many marriages maybe,
perhaps not even one. "Are you happy stranger?" "If so, what makes you
that way?"

Does your soul yearn to be eclipsed by another listlessly wandering heart?
Where do you reside O' soul? Contact Chicago or New Orleans, Seattle or
L.A.? Did we meet on the streets of Portland or Vegas? Was it in the U.S. or
Canada and beyond?

No! It was none of these. It was down at the mall, anywhere, world. We
met; we jockeyed; we contested, and both finally landed together on planet
earth. Take time to see the people there. The contact of one may be the

moment of fulfillment for the rest of your life. A stranger at our door or one you meet on the street. That stranger, obliquely hiding behind the mask, on that short lived encounter is one you must learn the rudiments of living with; the stranger may be you.

I love you with all of your secrets or any mask you wear

Dad

Dear Kids,

Re: How Successful are You?

The measure of a person is the measure of how far they have come from where they started. This shows where you have been. It sometimes gives a valuable clue to what you are.

Now let's look at the launching pad for all of us. We all start as a tabla rasa-a clean slate, upon which can be written on almost infinity life scripts The biological and anatomical givens seem to be limiting factors, but they are only limiting factors. They are only limiting if the recipient reacts in a limiting way to their environment. The person in this respect is the variable. He may be molded, sculpted or mixed in such a myriad of ways that virtually any shape and form is possible. Then, the real quest comes. How the form reacts to a flexible environment produces unrestricted permutations and combinations. What format we have is an infinite physical adoption meting on infinite environment array.

Out of this population are pulled as sampling units. We are separate people. Ours is to do where with all our will dictates. We are given the opportunity and responsibility to make choices which determine our fate or the events and consequences of our lives.

Thus, what you do and what you become is indubitably plastic. The certainty of your destiny lies simply in what you do with what you have got. That takes the pressure off. You can't run 100 miles an hour or a car at 200 miles per hour. Likewise you can't be expected to excel beyond those limits of physical endowment. The enigma! What are the limits for you or anyone else? You will only learn through your will.

What you become in life is measured as success when you accept yourself as you are, including all of your limitations and striving to become better. Certainly any accountability as such aptly measures a life well spent. No other standard will suffice except that which every child everywhere must learn from their parents. "Do the best that you can do!" You are your own standard bearer. Your journey in life demands you to:

1. Know what you got
2. Know your destination
3. Chart your course
4. Ask God for power
5. Let destiny lead the way

When you reach the last mile, rid yourself of all doubt and believe you have run your best race possible. Whatever your place, you have won the race.

Love,
Dad, your personal coach

Dear Kids,

Re: Sunshine

If darkness comes before dawn, why is the sun not shining?

If life is a bowl of cherries, why do I always get the pits? Life may not always be as dismal as this one popular outlook, but kids, I want to comment that we will not always be joyous, happy and free.

The ebb and flow of things creates a two step forward, one step backward walk. Just why does the sun not always shine? When it shines, why does it sometimes not shine for very long? Right after sobering up, I thought the upbeat feeling, of being on a *PINK CLOUD,*was here to stay.

What has happened to create a different picture? First, I sense a general dissatisfaction in the land. Having a significant impact on people, there is much turmoil in lives, especially those where troubles have been drowned with booze and/or various kinds of drugs.

If you are in a sea of trouble and all the other vessels you see are either shipwrecked, or badly damaged, the only view for you is wreckage. To survive with some semblance of health, you must somehow rise above the wreckage; you must also not let the owners of destruction prey on you. To set you aside and rise above these conditions, speak with God.

When you speak to God it will appear at times he has forsaken you. Your prayers will seem like vain repetitions falling on deaf ears. Darkness seems so pervasive, uncluttered by sound or sights, the vision of light at the end of the tunnel is just that is a vision. There is no light.

What is the meaning of the varied darkness, especially when it penetrates all plateaus of satisfaction that comes as you think the earthly paradise is greatest? Yet, surely, these experiences of the euphoric are short lived. A now-or-never predictably may be interrupted by chocolate covered clouds. They emit a darkening of the spirit from which the only known escape is through ascension to heaven.

I am trying to say that all things are not always bright and beautiful. Good times don't always last. They are often few and far between. What happens between the moments of sunlight? You guess it! You name it! The peril is sometimes more than I can bear. The emotional pain is as excruciating. I can only think it might be like crawling over broken glass. God! Kids, "it really hurts".

Because it hurts so much, I encourage you to fortify yourselves for those times which, for lack of better words are called generic depression. In other words build up protective devices during the good times so they will carry you over the bad times. These sustaining experiences can take on many forms. Prayer and meditation are the ones most frequently used ones and are probably the most universal. A quiet walk by the lake, a stroll in the moonlight with stars twinkling above, and a recompose to nature is a way of communing with the higher power and nature. The quiet solitude that comes through the harmony of a song, the sensitive lyrics telling the woes of heartache may help. More than anything else a quiet talk with a loving friend, whether it be during a long, drawn out evening or a short few moments over coffee.

Whatever makes you relax; whatever permits you to have strength; use these to get through the black time of darkness and despair. Use any method you can, anything you wish but one thing is absolutely certain, the bad things and ugly people don't go away. There are no places of paradise to escape to. Oh, the sun might warm it up more in Palm Springs, but the groceries cost more as every other convenience of life. Accept your plight wherever you are at, kids, and be glad in it. Your misery may not touch a candle to the next person's peril.

Love,

Dad

Dear Kids,

Re: Please Care About Self but not too much.

In a world emphasizing individualism and may the best man win, it is easy to forego the interests of others in the furtherance of self. This very delicate balance often finds one darting back and forth between these poles. At certain junctures in this Pandora of life swing others are prone to take a snapshot of us and place us somewhere along the pendulum. When enough shots are taken, a cluster forms providing a major configuration or what may even be called a constellation. Of most of these snapshots on the ego side we label one self-interests, selfish, self-willed, connected, etc.

When the picture image comes from the other side we tend to call them caregivers, philanthropists and other wonderful labels attached to those we revere for their sharing their resources including the more irreplaceable resources of all – one's time.

Keep care for yourself or give others care for their sake. The dilemma is answered in the world's greatest paradox which is TO RECEIVE YOU MUST GIVE AWAY.

This, my children, is a universal law. Collecting and hoarding of any resources is contrary to nature's law (God's immutable patterns). I can respond to the sharing of God's resources. By being responsible I can share myself and all that I possess. Listening to these words, however, does not confirm the rightness of our choices. To shovel the snow in -30 degrees may not have apparent return. Just remember when you do this your aging mother and fathers are exempt from doing these contemptuous things. The payoff is psychological.

Other dividends chosen are much more concrete, resulting from transactions of giving. We are told that we *reap what we sow*. Now if you sow anger or hatred, in some form this will come back to you sometime. Sowing love has the same effect.

Living in a world where your own ego is the centre of the universe and where you never give is going to create a life for you which is particularly brutish and selfish. It doesn't mean you must literally lay down your life for another or even forego personal resources to the extent your father does. It doesn't mean if you shovel an elderly neighbors walk you will someday get your own shoveled ten times; it does mean on the spiritual level of goodness you will know in your heart you have been good.

Contrasted to that you will likewise know in your heart that if you do things only for yourself and hoard your time and resources, your heart will suffer a constricted existence and it will not fly like an eagle so you will be free – free in the sense you feel a part of God's world and share the candidacy for remaining there forever.

Please learn to give, but only to your hearts desire.

Love,

Dad

Dear Kids,

Re: On Treasures

What treasures will you store?

It is both easy and difficult to protect our treasures. Notable as well is recognizing the many of these gems which through time take on different values. What may have been worth a lot when we were young may assume a great difference later; the value of what it was before diminished drastically. Some values, which hover at a high meta-physical level, may ascend to prime importance as the years wane away. Such things as compassionate sharing one's life with another, the ultimate expressions of law – the law of love – are not felt much by younger people or maybe be least understood.

The great peril is you and the glory it represents as God's gift to the world. Your being, the reflection of God through you, is a microcosm of the universe. Its essence is an image of God. You may call it what you wish, but it doesn't change what it is. You may even deny where it comes from on the very sustenance which sustains it, but to deny God and the power of God does not make it not be.

We humans are prone to hook labels to ourselves and live as though that is what we are. We may be more than we seem, more than mere labels. You are a great story by-line, a great piece of art, the most magnificent of all the sense can reveal, and then some.

You are more than you think you are. You are a pearl of worth beyond any comprehensive value. Your treasure is more than this. It is feelings of love and hate as one. It is being! No more feelings of inadequacy or inferiority.

How do you store up these treasures in heaven? You do it by knowing and loving God such that you want none other than to do his will. Pray, as you understand prayer, for knowing his will.

The treasure you have may not be of worldly acclaim but surely you will discover that it doth not corrupt. Constant vigilance to the pearl is not to focus on the pearl at all, but it's to focus on the cause of God.

Cause expressed in human form is will. Will to the cause of good which is love in its entire glory; look not toward a selfish motive to meet your own ends, but cast a selfless face to provide meaning in the lives of others. Your reward will be sure and steadfast. Let not your heart be troubled for the pearl will glow to radiate a warmth to all those who are around you.

The selfish pursuits of pleasure and vain petitions for worldly gain or fame have their own rewards. Seek a place in God's house and your reward will glow more than the pearl and be sweeter than honey.

Love,
Dad

Dear Kids,

Re: "If a job is worth doing, it is worth doing well"

Why do jobs well if you can do them half assed and get away with it? Many variations of this question exist along with a wide array of answers for each question. The variations I would actually write about are, "What jobs do you think you should do? "How well should you do the job (the task of your choice)?

Before getting into the philosophy of work, I'd like to tell you a little about my personal work habits. I am quick to admit that one's propensity for work is not a genetic endowment. We learn to work and later we work to learn. We learn to work for what we are exposed to: work models (especially parents), T.V., books, relatives and many more. Needless to say if the experiences are pro-work it will show in us. If much negates work and doing work well, we become prime candidates for welfare doling or quick job shifts. In other words, such people can't seem to hold down a job no matter what.

Well, I learned that work was not only important but valuable. Thus, in the main I cherish it. It has been very easy for me, then, to be a pretty "hard worker", ranging from milking the cows as their shit filled tails in your face, to bucking hay bales. I did it only rarely as a result of Dad's initiative. It was often boring riding the tractor all day, especially when the movies or trip to town would have been an easier softer way. Tread softly, but remember he who doesn't work, doesn't eat. Unless the Government baby-sits for us!

Now is there a philosophy related to work? Well! I think so. Either one works or they don't. If you have a job, you are likely responsible to finish it. Some greasy, grimy jobs are menial. No! They are downright distasteful. Is one a better person for doing clean jobs other than dirty jobs? The better person is one who does the job well and enjoys what he is doing.

It's not what you make, but being content doing it that counts. A shoe shiner can be eminently successful if he puts the heart and soul into shining shoes and make a masterpiece of it. A picker of prunes doesn't need to harvest the entire crop before the sun sets or pluck as many as the least worker, he only need put forth his best effort for the good of all. How do you the weary worker know the best effort and why should you believe the best is a desired mandate.

Answers come from deep within. Behind the bellybutton you will know!

Look Hard,

Dad

Dear Jenni,

Re: Don't be a Daddy's Girl Any More

Jenni, my first child, when you were born I experienced one of the happiest moments of my life. The hospital advised us that before we could bring you home, but we must pay the hospital fee first. Although I have joked about maybe leaving you there, I would have taken you for any price in the world.

What I say about my kid applies to all my children. As a matter of parental course, what I say about my children should apply to all children everywhere. What you say about your children should certainly keep me in understanding mine. Keeping this in mind, why do I say I don't want you to be a daddy's girl anymore?

My identification with you, my dear, was overdone. I wanted you to be a spitting image of me. This was despite my many character defects and ill fated insecurities and inferiority complex. Unfortunately you bought into, through learning things, these wanton wastes. Now you must spend the rest of your life digging yourself out of this carnal skullduggery of all those disclaimers to be a healthy human in a psychological sense.

We should never have kept the ringing refrain going, "You are a special girl" We should have meant we accept you as an average and loved precious daughter of ours.

Jeff, the same ideal was directed toward you, but with different results. I wanted you to be the model son, despite the need to have you be not only the best athlete imaginable. The offshoot was that you were a superior athlete than what I was in my day, but also you were a better scholar.

If we were referring to countables like test scores and batting averages it would be one thing. I cannot escape, because of my overbearing concern for you, to get into the area of personal habits, habits of personal hygiene, and social proclivities to that standard upon which my own life was built which lacked much. This created a dilemma, a monstrous demon. Is there ever any right way or wrong way to do something?

Some of us are people pleasers, others of us don't give a damn what others think. So whether it be in sports, academics, work, religion, politics, or etc., don't attune yourself to the universal conscience. It is best described by the Buddha, at least as belief is referred to as consciousness.

Buddha
Believe nothing because a so called wise man said it.
Believe nothing because a belief is generally held.
Believe nothing because it is written in ancient books.
Believe nothing because it is said of being of divine origin.
Believe nothing because someone else believes it.

Believe only what you yourself judge to be true.
"Believe not what your dad tells you to believe."

Love,

Dad

Dear Kids,

Why Did I Win the Rocky Mountain Conference Half - mile (1959)?

As a young child I was a nuisance or rambunctious adolescent, I was a fighter believing that one achieves ascent and access by the instinct of dominance. The street was the testing ground for the universal law of maleness. Conquering your opponent can be accomplished on the field of battle, or in the locker room. My battlefield was the world. Everything and everyone was my opponent. The most formidable of all, the bottle, ultimately conquered me.

I learned some lessons from those fifty years. I was the R.M.C. half mile championship to be better than the next guy. Now I use the lessons of life to not have to conquer everyone, but to live in a world where doing O.K.! Is it good enough? Getting a Ph.D. was my own attempt to conquer by commanding a spot in the occupational world. I came! I conquered! I fell!

Downward I spiraled. Then with a big splash my innards splattered shedding 45 years of life with a tormenting pane. The road back is slow and difficult – but sure. Now I pass along to you kids, "straight is the way and narrow is the gate and few there are that find it".

Love,

Dad

Dear Kids,

Re: Living in the Moment

It has been awhile since I have written. I guess because of those feelings that people reach a point in their lives when they realize they can't go it alone. I must keep in contact for all intents and purposes my delusion is that I have the ability to make it alone.

What rays are in our lives when the despair comes from sheer age where fear leads to that quiet desperation when we are caught in two worlds- yesterday and tomorrow? Without being able to go backward or forward, one can be caught in abyss of the moment. Living in the moment is a trick played on us by crazy world. "Step right up and a quarter will give you three chances to win." We have already used all our quarters. The bank will not loan us anymore, the collateral does not buy into the future, so each in his own is caught in the present. Not like a lightning flash or a thought that goes to sleep for awhile, reality is that we must navigate today and only today, -one day at a time.

Truth and its consequences pass. At dawn? At dusk? The nearest I can determine is it begins with an event and ends when that event is finished. Interrupted events don't make days, they make colossal gaps in consciousness. What fills the gaps is the continuous bombardment of present with thoughts of yesterday and tomorrow. The present or now is this moment which is curious. Impact??? Impact??? Impact??? We must ask the question, "What is the composition of the moment?"

What is a moment in time? Does it have a beginning and end? I think not, it just is. The morning comes only from dating the immediate events surrounding it. It's like the dating of an artifact. You analyze that which surrounds it and realize the artifact is exactly the same as its immediate surroundings. It is a moment in time and it is also an eternity, just as we understand the physical and spiritual worlds.

Love,
Dad

Dear Kids,

Re: On Understanding

Awareness in its most general sense is recognition of an object or event in experience. This is often referred to as perception for humans. When humans willfully react to what they become aware of by taking the object into account and in this process subjectively pursue action.

Becoming aware and acting on it is the essence of life. The nature of my awareness context is life's ultimate pursuit. For example, the question "What is the most important thing in life?" takes on significance in the context of the person's awareness and the situation into which it is found.

A, father who for many years, has yearned for an intimate relationship with his son may sense ultimate joy when they both walk the dog around their favorite lake on a pleasant fall evening and hear his son say, "Dad, what do you think is the most important thing in life?"

The father may or may not understand the motivation or experiential base for his son's question. He knew intimately what that same question meant to himself many years ago. Part of the heart's delight came from the question being asked in the first place. A certain amount of trust must be a prerequisite for such an intimate question. Even though I don't have the answer, I can offer some suggestions which might serve as tentative but reliable provision.

Would it not seem less obtrusive in life I suggest the most important thing in life is life itself. The stuff which makes the flowers grow; the energy that brings wrinkles on grandmother's face; even when green grass and trees turn vivid orange and chocolate brown; and the workings of millions of twinks of nature demonstrate the transforming power of the stuff of which I speak.

Human life is only one version of life that we know. Its versions are edited only by each one of us. Thus, as I tell my son what I see as the most important thing in life; it is screened and processed only through my eyes. As my son knows, my life is not entirely innocent.

My innocence and lack of it has given my soul a penchant to embellish its grasp of love.

If life is most important; love rivals it as a close second. Love, much like life, defies symbolic denotation. I spend time with my dog; we don't symbolize, but I love my dog. I think she loves me. Would I be so silly as to ask an eschatologist to prove me wrong? Or right of that matter. No, I think not.

Life and love are the big two. From these absolutely any and all significant proportions flow.

The answer to my son's question, then, is rather simple. He asked me, "Dad, what is the most important thing in life."

My child, "It is to love and to live".

Love,

Dad

Dear Kids,

Re: On Health

Once your health gets to the point where it is manageable, it is time to maintain yourself at the level of health which you choose.

The maintenance mode might be slightly different for each of you. Lying differences aside some common elements appear in a profile of an archetype of all humans' health.

Somewhat before the end of life, any 30 - 50 yr. old doesn't have an ecstatic life. They reach a career peak at about 45. Then they become secure in the face of job seniority. Life is not terribly happy nor the blatant opposite. Enjoying social encounters and calling one a social drinker. Positive about a social - religious viewpoint of life! Enjoys being right and excels to make leisure work and work to have leisure.

Love,

Dad

Dear Kids,

Re: On Taking a Break

I don't know about you, but as for me it's time to take a mental health break. Like always, those of us trained in the social sciences think we have to define our terms before communication is possible. Little do we realize that it impedes communication as much as it enhances it?

Let's play the definition game for a moment and follow along in its leading. Time, being the lapse between point A and B, is both subjectively relative and constant. A day may sometimes seem like a year and a year may sometimes seem like an instant. With the passing of time, events happen in nature. We include natural and social events. Concerns of mental function are so numerous it is difficult to note precisely those things that are minds. However, we may refer to cognitive abilities which make healthy or unhealthy people.

A mental health break, then, refers to the time necessary to either improve health or to make it maximally effective.

I choose the latter!

The 64 dollar question is how to accomplish this. Roundly and soundly, it cannot be done by oneself introspectively. Happiness may be an inside job, but only by focusing on something from the outside.

The therapy I choose is to take time to do nothing.

I have a book with this title. I will loan I to you.

It's a good read!

Love,

Dad

Dear Jenni and Jeff,

Re: Money Management

I have been thinking recently where your mom and I have failed in raising you. In most respects you both have turned out just great, but there is one area that all of us in our family have been sloppy and negligent. This is in the area of money management. We have never taught either of you about budgets because we have been fortunate in our lives to have a generous (in my opinion) amount of money to spend.

Both of you don't necessarily share this point of view. You have expressed concern over not having what you would like. Thus I am proposing that each one of you work out a rough budget. Put down all categories of areas you need for - car, insurance, gas, clothes, tuition, etc. Keep track of what you spend. Include in your budget a rough guess of what you spend for food, clothing and shelter. As long as you are our children (we would never charge you for these – but you should become aware of what it is on paper anyway).

Just opening pocket books by parents is irresponsible and poor judgment.

I know both of you are going to reject this proposal but if you do, there is a kicker. If you don't prepare a budget for yourselves, your mom and I are going to do it for you. So, since I think we will be much more generous to approving your budget, I hope you take this seriously. A budget tells us where we are at financially. Both of you have experience in the big, bad, world – and I think it's time to put that experience into practice.

Let it be known that we are not the best teachers about budgets so let's look at this as an exciting learning experience. If the truth were known – and I believe it would be our well being in the next few years will be due to working harmoniously as a kind of mini-business, or society.

Why don't we make it work so everyone involved can benefit most for what God has gracefully given - us our resources with our time and talent. After all, a few minutes each day could be the difference between lives of contentment as opposed to disappointment.

Any questions we can discuss in our next family meeting - which everyone is expected to attend. Your co-operation will be greatly appreciated.

PLEASE HELP OUR FAMILY AND YOU

Love,

Dad

Dear Kids,

Re: Since You Were Here

While you were gone, you might wish to know what's up at home. Wherever go in this world and whatever you may do while gone, I wonder if you think about us as much as we at home think about your being gone.

It probably doesn't make any difference whether you were a days drive away, or a days flight on the fastest jet liner, your absence was essentially the same. Jeff, when you called from Tel Aviv, all I could think of was scud missiles. You're spending Christmas alone, that is without your family, your birthday past and when we didn't have our family dinner together, plus your candles burning dim without you to blow them out; we missed you. Jenni, your being in Idaho made me a bit envious of you. Jeff, you had gone to places I had only dreamed of and a bit scared to think about. I still wondered how you were.

Jeff, could I ever know how you felt as you walked some of the same country Jesus walked? You lived at a different time than the pioneers of the west? What am I really scared of? If you know how you are and where you are at the moment, of my pensive frenzy should pass. I knew that you were mine only because of our common feelings.

I realized once and for all your life was yours and I could never own it. For all intents -and- purposes I knew you had come of age and I could never keep you in my own time tunnel; a vision of time past I could no longer feel. I could no longer be the patriarch of your life. I could only become to you "you own father", perhaps similar to our **father** who art in heaven, I had by the choice of reality to give you away to let you have a life "mate" or vision. I could not control anymore. You were the author of your own life. I couldn't tell you to go to the doctor when you were sick, or to say your prayers when you were depressed. I couldn't tell you where to go and what to do.

Was there anything left for me, other than to live in the nostalgic notion you were symbolically in my arms. All that was left for me was to wait for you to visit home. It wasn't ever a welcome home, it was how nice for you to come and visit awhile. My agony was your ecstasy. Your life was your own. What was left of mine?

To receive your love and pass it on!

Pass your love to a lost soul,

Dad

Dear Kids,

Re: Knowing About You

When you leave home, let us know where you are and where you are going. This letter is addressed to whatever kid claims me as their father. This could be our two biological children, or it could be the two kids my wife and I became legal guardians of when they were eleven and twelve years old. This is now many years later.

The fate of these children would forever be unknown. If we had not "adopted" these children their fate could be absolutely anything possible – foster homes, or virtually on the street in their teens – or whatever. We eradicated our fears by bringing you into our home which became a blessing beyond what words can tell.

Although we don't know – we can only speculate on what your lives would have been without us; you are indelibly imprinted on us so that you know what it was like with us. At least we know what our part of your lives we helped mold.

We could have lived without you before we met you, but can't live without you now. Some very direct and pointed questions come to mind as we grieved over Jennifer left home, unannounced and secretive while leaving. It was so easy for you. All you had to do was wait until we went to church Sunday morning; load your things and leave. Who would be the wiser? We weren't. We forgave you immediately. Now both of you, Julie and Jennifer, are gone. Girls we cherish your time with us.

Here are some of the questions my wife and I must ask here in our quiet moments of desperation as we try to answer to each other, "Did we fail?" The conversation would go something like this, Dad - "Why did you decide to leave home?"

Kid - "Because I wanted to move in with my boyfriend."

Dad and Mom - "Did we fail?" Is this what we parented for"? We thought we were living in the olden days. What were the olden days like, we mused.

Dad & Mom thought, "Why did we ever decide to raise the kids in the first place? Did we really deserve the excruciating pain of this moment?" I guess so because we learned to love unconditionally.

Love, Dad and Mom

P.S. Conundrums all of them and many more, I, the dad, tell myself "that's life". What did my wife tell herself as she cried the days away? Why did such a bad thing happen to such good people? You'll never know girls just what you have done. Angry, hurt, and surely what we know about what is ahead for you. We know! You will find out sooner or later one way or another. We will forever forgive you for surely you will know not worry if your own children make similar choices.

Dear Jeff,

Re: Wanting you to stay home

I have found it so much easier to work things out – apologies or otherwise – by talking things out face-to-face, but I am got the distinct impression you weren't going to permit this to happen. I'm glad I later found out different.

So here goes the best I am capable of. I am, of course, like every other human I have ever known, things at times come out of my mouth that are not really meant, or they are said to try and persuade you in an awkward way; different from that perceived.

You have heard me say a number of times, "What Peter says about Paul says more about Peter than it does about Paul". Well, the fact is – in no way do I consider you a bum – although the Peter/Paul principle seems to apply.

Often I get little bits and pieces mixed up. I have been very distraught because of your wanting to leave again so soon. You mentioned on the way from Calgary that we should sit down and have a talk. I was hoping we could do that fairly often – but it looks like this will not occur this trip home.

I have been trying to argue in a way for you to stay home for awhile. I have no right to try and control your life. I do have a right to tell you I want to get to know you.

I know a so called friend triggered an attitude which I jumped on and pre-judged you for. However, all the specifics and details could create an argument ad infinitum. I don't want to argue, fight, or have bad feelings. I tried to tell you this person was no good, then, and I up and let him create a big wedge between us. He was a sociopath!, so why would I let him say something which would influence me over what my son says? I didn't even give you a chance to tell me you had called from Calgary. I just wanted you to stay home.

Jeff, you are just as welcome to our family resources as I am. I'm sorry for the cutting remarks about no money. Your trip makes me proud that my son had such courage. Any small amount of money we helped with was minuscule. I am not fair in bringing that, or cars, or anything, into our arguments.

You may have your "grubstake" anytime you want it. Just let Mom aware and we will get it right away.

By the way, Jeff, Mom worries and loves you so much. You should not find her at fault because of my sins.

Someday I hope you will forgive me and we can treat each other like two adults. We sort of missed that in my alcoholic years. I sure hope we can reconcile sometime. I do love you – despite what appearances may see.

I will pray for us. God knows I need it.

Love,
Dad

Dear Kids,

Re: Drive Your Own Bus

Every once in awhile; life permits us to coast along. We tend to just put in a minimum of effort and expect the maximum in return. These are the good times when, while resting on our laurels, someone else is doing the work for us. Life cannot always be so conveniently easy. Not only is it necessary to muster enough effort to finish a task, but we must exert ourselves simply enough to say we are part of the task.

What if we can get by letting others assume our responsibility because we don't feel like taking responsibility ourselves? Performance is assessed and validated through the eyes of others. I am more concerned how you kids look at yourselves through your own eyes. How do you stack up in your own view?

As a parent, I often ask myself this question. When my kids play not their own personal part, I say what did I do wrong as a parent to bring about this state of affairs. Nor do I face reality. I can't be responsible for what happens to another person, even though I would be willing to stake my life on the outcome if that would tip the balance.

However, there are occasions when laying one's life down would be foolhardy. For example, if the God given talent of a child saw that child performing at the level of 100 I.Q. when their I.Q. is 150 or higher something is array somewhere. Did I go wrong as the parent in this dilemma? What if I have a child who has a 110 I.Q, and through hard work and discipline is able to graduate from university? Which one will I recognize?

It seems unequivocal, if you wish to get somewhere, you must decide whether to drive your own bus to the destination or ride with someone else, or not go anywhere at all.

Life is a cruel teacher sometimes. It doesn't give us a second choice. We simply miss the bus and there aren't any more buses running. We can be left standing in the middle of nowhere, wanting to go somewhere, and we have no more opportunities to go.

About the same thing as saying that if you make your bed you must lie in it. Life is real, kids. Don't take it for granted. It is ruthless and thorough in its lessons to us. If you are taught a lesson by life, treat the experience tenderly. Whatever it takes to redress a major mistake should be pursued vigorously and gently. It is these testy moments that are the difference between a winner and loser. Certainly it teaches humility.

If my own humility can serve as example, I must advise you.

Count your losses, pick yourself up after mistakes, and either vigorously pursue another chance, or an alternative. The life you save may be your very own. You may find you can drive your own bus, if you know how to fix a flat tire.

You will surely know what it means when the tire hits the road!

Love,

Dad The great tire fixer

Dear Kids,

Re: On Celebrations

Let's celebrate! What do you say? Any numbers of occasions give rise to lofty celebrations. Christmas, New Years, Birthdays, Valentines Day, all of these and more! Among the more notable in my book is Groundhog Day. Now the name of the day is not important – what is important is the meaning of the Holiday. One could say the observation of the shadow of the ground hog himself can tell the weather for sometime in the future.

Well, ground hog day means a day for celebration to me. My birthday is on this day, but not my belly button birthday. The birthday I am talking about takes on special significance. It is that day denoting my last day of drinking, my A.A. celebration. Each year on a specified date, a member and others if one is fortunate enough to have those who care; recognition is made for each year of sobriety. The first year is very important.

I remember standing before my A.A. fellows and saying what amounted to me as my philosophy of life. "Why has the world passed me by?" Tears were easy to come as I tried to answer this question. The truth never comes out; the world had just slipped by me. I found the world again, many years later, inside myself.

You will too if you look hard enough.

Dad

Dear Kids,

Re: On Finding a Job

What do you do when the economy is bad? Recessions don't mean much to a lot of people. To others it is the heading in a newspaper. Then there are the others, people like yourselves trying to get a start in the work world. Many - out there - are trying to find a job; any job will do for them.

Looking for a job is one thing. Trying to find a job when none are available is quite another. Overcoming this difficulty by accomplishing this task equates to like finding a needle in a haystack. At least, however, when you are searching for the needle the activity tends to prevent ennui.

Job searching may be somewhat different for different people. There are listings that come up in flyers, the employment office, newspaper, word of mouth, and so on. When you see an advertised job, even as they rarely come up, you play a game of juggler by trying to match up your person with the job.

Then, you send in your application knowing full well that many others have done the same. If you are lucky enough to get an interview; you wait in anticipation on pins and needles for that formidable day. Then, often the agonizing hour of the interview comes in a few days. It seems like weeks go by until you hear. Expectantly you wait for the mailman every day. Then, the day comes and you are afraid to open the letter. Of course you have opened such letters before. This one may be different and there may be a chance that you can land this job.

Finally, the letter comes. Warily you slowly open it. You peek at it. It begins. We are sorry to inform you, but the position has been filled. Why wasn't I a more qualified candidate? Sinking back into my chair I tell myself, "I need a few days to regroup then I will try again".

The tragedy of this episode happens not once, not twice, but many, many times. The loser is the person's ego. Finally, strength gives out and you find yourself at the offices of social services. You know the rest of the story.

So the message I have for you kids, **is persevere**. A job or a career may not be quickly forthcoming. You may wish to appreciate the roof over your head a comfortable bed to sleep in and food in the refrigerator. Maybe, just maybe tomorrow will be different – things may turn around in the economy. Jobs may open up. Perhaps your long years of study will pay off. You may get a job you were trained for. Finally, after years of paying back the student loan; after years of keeping your nose to the grindstone; you may sigh and say to yourself. My dream has been fulfilled; I am now where I have always wanted to be. Then a sudden jolt comes. You are awakened by this startling jolt and you say to yourself. Good God, another day. **This to shall pass!**

Things could be worse,

Dad
And you believe, Dad

Dear Kids,   April 8, 1992

Re: Getting Along As Adults

So many times I wrote you letters trying to offset our mutual difficulties. On the time of celebrating your 22nd birthday, I wanted to write a letter celebrating your victories. It has been a long and tortuous struggle for us to get where we are today. Of course, we don't have anything near a perfect father - son relationship, and often what we have been through together; the scars of days gone by will probably always show. Nevertheless, it feels so good for us to get along amiably as two adults can.

Of recent years, I have thought the ideal world is to love kids unconditionally, but I must confess I have never been able to attain the ideal. My heart has always desired a professional life for you, for occupational and economic success. When your mother and I are long gone we want you to be secure. All the money, security material, well-being, or anything else will only be a shadow to how one relates to God and fellow man. It is important to care; I have found that growth comes by sharing with others.

It is much too late to try and be a moral entrepreneur with you, Jeff. I am glad that some of your own values have stood out above others, for example, to get through school rather than have a fancy car. I know you have had to fight for your rights and your struggle has not been easy.

Now that the rough years are over and you are about ready for post-graduate studies, I do want you to be aware of the full-fledged backing of the family for this. I mean this in a supportive and financial way. Together we will get where you want to go. This is an absolute promise. This is our dream. And we will see it fulfilled. If it had not been for problems years ago we would have been home free, but please know we are behind you.

I hope this birthday can be celebrated with joy. I hope you appreciate life and the gifts God has given you. He surely has blessed you with distinct talents. May you always use them for his will to be done in your life? He surely has blessed us for you to be a member of our family. May we always thank him by always loving you? I thank you for being my son!

Love,

Your Dad

Dear Kids,

Re: Some Things We Pick and Choose in this World. Others are not in Our Grasp.

I just found out that I am the victim of another physical ailment which is both unwelcome and uninvited. I seriously thought when I recovered from the nuisance aspect of alcoholism; I had received my earthly due. Now I can add diabetes to the asthma, manic-depression and alcoholism. I write, however, not to cry and whine but to carry a word of hope. A mutual hope we may share and arising from the traumas of our lives that we have over come and conquered.

Illness, in whatever guise it appears, is not welcome to those seeking a wholesome life. Even with illness, everyone can be the best they can be or live the best of all possible worlds.

I have seen so many people simply cave in or shrivel to desperation through illness. They can't seem to adapt; they complain and become so reactive that illness rules them rather than them ruling the illness.

So like the other illnesses which have been my fate, I will try to conquer diabetes. I realize I probably will not live as long because of this the quality of my life must offset the lost time. To eat a sugar free diet from now on, to be advised to walk at least 3 times a week, to monitor my blood sugars seem tough as they are written, but they are only stumbling blocks if one makes them out to be.

Well, what's this to do with you? Jeff, more will happen to you in life than just having asthma. Jenni, you have already had your share and the biggie which you got from me, manic depression, will be with you for the rest of your life.

I know it has been a horrible struggle – the **stigma** and all!

Don't let these be your stumbling blocks. Do what you have to do – take your medicine. You can have a full and productive life in every way possible by treating your illnesses with respect and dignity. Discouragement is the flip side of hope. Be hopeful. Let the synergy of your hearts be more of a healing balm than sickness.

God bless and take your pills.

WALK RIGHT THROUGH YOUR MALADIES

Please don't live in the problems! Live in the solutions. I have and it works.

Love,

Dad

Dear Kids,

Re: If You Break the Rules, You Must Pay the Consequence

We are empowered to choose and we have much latitude for doing this. Even so there are specific and sometimes vague limits serving as boundaries for our decisions. A seed bed and boundaries for rules are parents and their offspring.

They, of course, come in many sizes and shapes; each in its own way provides different needs for its members. For its survival, a family has its rules for members to live by. No rules mean total chaos. Rigid rules establish conformism – in rigid form - totalitarianism.

Rules are made for the betterment of its members so tasks can be accomplished collectively which cannot be done alone. The family is also its own little finishing school preparing the initiates and untutored their place in the larger world.

In society, we learn there are rules to live by and rules to break, when a contestant feels he can get away with it. Telling the truth and keeping a commitment are veritable bastions for sound personal conduct. They also make it possible for the unit to survive.

In-as-much as a variety of rules can be broken; numerous consequences for their violation may be invoked. However, the punishment does not always match the crime. Modern day parents do not practice the law of lex talionis. Ours are often judgment calls, and no standard bearer can proclaim any thorough innocence. They may try - rightness.

I am left with a whole barrage of dirty tricks which I am quick to recognize and verbalize. This onslaught is counterclaimed by a smattering of opposing deeds being a pale shadow of their diametric. In short, I have spoken to your debits and hardly echo the good.

No wonder you defied me. I cast myself into a black parental abyss. Is it any wonder that at times your departure from the rules startled my sense of propriety and justice? Yet, you have created a realm outside of this. You have appealed to the universal wanderlust within. So he's gone – she's gone, they've all gone away from the tyranny of the past to the freedom of the present.

Now the present makes me capitulate, not once but many times. I resound and say, "I don't know! I just don't know." All I can do is act and hope you are not harmed by my action, I may be wrong, or you may be, but in either case does it really matter?" Parent and child may differ in their views. They, like honest people, may differ. They may still love and live together. I hope you will realize this some day, too.

Love,
Dad

Dear Kids,

Re: On Shopping

"When you buy something, make sure you need it."
How many of us in this world purchase something followed by the intense remorse of whether we did the right thing. The remorse may be intense or slight. I even wonder sometimes if there is a correlation between the cost of an object and our doubtful feelings after.

Cars, for example, are a big purchase for most of us. Buying them used makes our decisions more vulnerable. The only difficulty with new ones is whether you have enough money or not and whether perhaps the money could be better used elsewhere, perhaps something for the kids.

I have, on occasion, purchased used vehicles, and heavy feelings have prompted me to get out of the deal, once when I was drinking and another time ten years sober. The latter was this morning. When anyone, anywhere, puts a doubt in my head about the merit of a deal, I can't sleep easily. Late yesterday evening, then, when I made a $200 down payment on a car, I was, I thought, comfortable with the decision until your mom starts nagging me about not consulting her about the deal. One thought led to another, until I started questioning the whole deal myself. The cost, the mileage, was based on fraud.

The die was cast, when a doubt is put in my mind the fire is lit and continues to rage out of control until it is somehow abated. In this case, after my mind had raved long enough, I got up early this morning, called the guy I bought the car from and politely asked if I could get out of the deal if I paid him handsomely for his time. He didn't appear to hesitate that much.

When I got to his place a few minutes later he was mumbling about me being the third person this week that had made a deposit on the car and backed out.

Not thinking about the logic of this, I quietly peeled 3 twenties off the 200 I had given him – $50 I had said over the phone and asked him if he had $10 – No, he said, "I said will $60 be okay and with his hesitation I mumbled that $40 would be over $30 an hour for his trouble. He agreed. The contract was torn up. I breathed a sigh of relief.

It was an expensive lesson, but cheaper than the doubts that surely would have followed had the original decision been carried through.

So, who knows what kind of deal to make? At least I hope you are confident of yourselves and are not only comfortable with your choice, but will be able to sleep with them later. Then perhaps those you love can support you in your decision, too. After all it is not much reason for misunderstanding.

Love,
Dad

Dear Kids,

Re: Dealing with Depression

What do you do when you're depressed, other than commit suicide?

Life has many welcome and unwelcome surprises for us. Some short lived, others prolonged. Among those which go or stay are what I term "fits" of depression. The onset of uncontrollable melancholy is as close to anything as a demonic gift.

I am not even going to try and describe such a state. Words do not give a clear picture anyway. It is unique to the beholder and yet it is understandable for all who have experienced this genre. As I sit here in a blue state today, I write as one inspired to tell you how to get through these times.

The number one way for curing depressions is to nip it in the bud. I think that calling an end to it all may be the only reasonable thing to do. One must somehow cut their losses. When the pain is more than one can take, it must be eradicated.

One can never always know the best course of action. To assist me, I called on my three most trusted friends to help me answer the question, "Should I commit suicide?"

One said yes, with hesitation or qualification. I went to my best friend of longest term. She said if you do, you will miss out what you have counted on all your life, the marriage of your daughter and son watching the unfolding of their lives and ensuing happiness.

She continues, "What would I do about being alone for the rest of my life?" – "I would have to sell the house quickly", she said. I weighed these things carefully.

My last friend's situation was particularly suited to my relentless pursuit of life's meaning and purpose. She did not preach a sermon to me. She showed me. Imbibed by the elixir of the ages, it took strong will to tell her I was there to talk straight with her.

We talked straight. I asked her if we should commit suicide together. She said she desperately needed me. She may have been conning me, but what she said made a lot of sense. I know that I can't get along without her. Yes! We are lost in the wilderness of or emotions. Can we find our way out together, or is the blind leading the blind? Although I think I am close to the perimeter of discovery. I may be closer to the rim than she is, but aren't we both searching for the same destination.

Friend, Thanks for the wise counsel

Dad

MORE MUSINGS

Bonding in Adulthood
&
Hope for the Future

Dear Kids,

Re: Let's Do Something – Preferably Together

My invitation, half-hearted as it is, must necessarily be two invitations. No longer can I relate to you as kids with whom I perform a ritualistic obligation of parent child context. Ours was an intimate sharing of loneliness – time spent without each other instead of a father bonding with daughter and separation from daughter and father bonding with son and separation from son. We failed! Our lives are not over today, but maybe will be before the full impacts of our letters settle firmly in your hearts. I would like to go with you. I must express my concerns to you separately.

Jenni, my eldest, and you, Jeff, who may look at the others bonding with little interest, I confess with open and contrite spirit that both of you lacked a soul father until you had passed the age of initiation into adulthood. Only you know deep within what it's like to have a "father in absentia, one in body, and not in spirit."

We were united for awhile, Jenni. When you were a little girl, I was your "bud". At a very tough time in your life, we drifted apart. I was absorbed in my job and the drinking life. You were absorbed in the trauma (vagaries) of growing up in a hostile environment. The result was less estranged than it was neglect. In listing direction in my life, I lost contact with you.

Jeff, I guess the truth is, I was never a real father to you. I always saw you as a boy who was supposed to excel in everything he did from the first awkward moment of your standing at the plate and trying to hit the baseball, to the times you struggled in your own mind to be a national football league star. I have followed your sports career passionately with keen disinterest. This "dis" part is because I didn't follow it by seeing your struggles, your disappointments and your triumphs. Now let me put it in perspective – to tell it the way it was and is.

As a budding sports figure I, a mere 5'6" - 135 lbs., I had these great attributes going for me, heart and desire. One of my Graceland coaches mentioned once that had I the body of one of their more renowned athletes, I surely would have been All American! Such fantasies require their own unique death and burial.

But alas! I was reincarnated in my son. Here was someone who had more heart and more desire than me. Life with its ordeals cancelled out your sport career, before its due time of maturation. Be it engraved on your trophy of life, Jeff, your heart's desire was bigger than mine. I wonder perhaps if its size was not for the same reason he grew, to fill a gap – a real void left – because there was an absolute scarcity of bonding between me and my dad. If I could live life a second time around, it would include a relationship with my dad.

Hopefully, the remaining years of my life will find a resurgence of my "dad instinct" so I can get to know all my children, including J.J. and Julie. Bonding is such a contemporary word. Permit me to say that what's in my heart is to try and get to know you, and be able to be there when you need someone to talk to. Maybe, even, sometimes you might perhaps listen to me drone on, not only to let you know how tough the dad business is, maybe even sharing a tear or two to anticipate what one day, may be your fate, of having children of your own.

If you do and I sincerely hope you do because of the immeasurable pleasure they bring, please treat them delicately for they will be very special, very special indeed. I know because you proved this to me.

Love to my kids,

Dad

Dear Kids,

Re: Let's Play Catch!

I'm sorry I didn't have time to play **I had to go to work**. I know it's not just a matter of intellectual curiosity on your part to know what I mean by this when I have not held my teaching post for twelve years, or so. Your contempt is further demonstrated as if teasingly, but what I sense as your felt intent when you say, "You really don't have a job". I am not an O.K. person too – jobless and all - when your mother argues rather emphatically that she too knows, "that I really don't work or have a job".

In-as-much as who I am and what my life is about has been my source of being through my work for 12 years and probably will be until I die. I am going to try and make a feeble but last ditch effort in this small treatise to help you understand coming from the inner depths of my being why I deserve to say I work, too.

Job & work! Accomplish them and you get paid. For the life of me, I can't see this as all there is to a life of work. After all, people work to have fun, play at sex, they work to make themselves work; most of all they get a reward for their effort.

Now I want to write about living a life in such a way that everything is work or conversely everything is play, or some other thing - or whatever - but that all of activity has value.

First of all, I submit that when anyone does anything useful for self or for others, it can be classed as work. In any connectedness of ideas, we cannot forfeit that great chain of being, hence, useful may be defined as a state coming about when one's activities make the world a better place than before the activity was consummated.

Whoever, indeed, would be presumptuous enough to think, then, that a noble man who answers the phone to talk indeterminately based on the desire of the caller, drive – upon demand – anyone for an 1-1/2 hour ride to detox treatment centre, go to a whole bunch of A.A. meetings a week, do almost any odd job requested, mend the broken heart of a lover forlorn, sit in a bar while a grown man cries his heart out over the fear and despair in his life, drive 200 miles to pick a stranded friend up at the airport, and finally, listen and listen for hours to hear the troubled pour their heart out to you – these and many more are part of my job description.

Examine my portfolio. Trust to me the credit that I know my work, my business, my chosen profession. I am a skilled artisan, honed to a very fine edge. All this – or much of it at least – comes from on the job training, from the school of hard knocks.

I have fed other people's hungry hearts so much my own wounds have festered and not healed! As I sit here writing to you, I am physically, mentally, and emotionally exhausted. Just last night I witnessed in a bar fight equal to the L.A. riot. Another observer, a nice A.A. friend of mine enjoys the revelry as she drank glass after glass of beer.

Clinging to the notion that life is worthwhile and people are good, I must tell you how it's about time for me to go to work so I will be closing soon. I am going to see my psychiatrist and I will be asking him to help me gain my sanity. I am going to see if I can get on the ward in the hospital so I can rest up. I'm the doctor. I fix people, but nobody fixes me.! My strength is gone. I am "shrunk" as much as possible. I must recoup.

Please! For God's sakes can't you understand there's more to life than getting a pay check, to putting in 8 hours to say you have a job! I work so hard at my job that I have neglected you kids. Please understand when I must go to work my motive is strong, stronger than life itself. My job is living. Living is my work. Please understand I am important, too.

Why do I do these things?

I do what I do because I must. Must I really? This, my general appraisal, constitutes my personal theory of motivation – set through picking up bits and pieces from a variety of life experiences plus immersion in human behavioral approaches.

Love,

Dad

Dear Kids,

Re: By What Shall Ye Know Them?

One of life's interesting experiences is to observe the world of shoppers. Their obsessive compulsive behavior, often erratically unpredictable, arouses my curiosity enough to pose the ultimate challenge. Assuming no time limitations or any other restrictions for that matter, if the opportunity were yours to obtain anything of wealth or prestige in the world, what would you include in your shopping list? Travel and riches? Fame or fortune? Honor and prestige? What a list I might make. I introduce the message of this letter this way because I have found that one can value and cherish only a limited breadth of concerns and things.

Now one of these things that I value from my inner being is what now is a blue and white 1971 Ford truck. Most folks would find it valueless and others a mere few hundred dollars. It's mine. It's not for sale and I treat it with respect.

A demonstration of how I treat it is – the recent paint job, done for about $200 but a whole bunch of personally invested hours. Let me clear up the mystery. That truck was my dad's before he died. It sat in mom's yard for some time with no clear idea as to what to do with it. When I expressed an interest in it, my mom gave it to me. It has become my most prized possession. It's not the value of the product that is important, it's the meaning attached to it.

Thus, when on two separate occasions, my daughter and her boyfriend used it as a junk hauler and my son loaded our fishing boat improperly in it, damage was done to my new paint job. I was heartbroken.

Thus, we know people by what they possess. I don't have many possessions of the world, but my old truck is just as valuable as a brand spanking new one to me.

My parental advice for you children is this, when you borrow, use, rent, or utilize the property of anyone else in the world, treat it as though it is your own.

Even in the social world, always follow the grandma principle. Treat every one as though they are your friend. Follow these principles to their fullest and your lives will be immeasurably enriched.

Love,

Dad

P.S. If you ever borrow anything from someone, return it in better condition than when you took it. For example, don't return a vehicle with the gas tank empty or even the same as you received it.

Dear Kids,

Re: "Come Fly with Me!"

When Jenni was twenty four, Jeff was twenty one, Julie was sixteen and J.J. was fifteen your mother and I took a holiday. For the first time since you were born, or when you came to live with us we took a little holiday. We flew to Vancouver and bussed to Victoria in a car rented in Seattle.

I can't recount anything spectacular happening on this trip, which I have dubbed as our "honeymoon". It was hardly a honeymoon. We did get accustomed to hanging around together. We enjoyed going to tourist traps, eating crab legs, the most expensive meal of all times, was a pleasure.

The bright light of this little excursion with the past was our dip down into Seattle to have dinner with Stan and Chris. Yesterday afternoon, I got the brainstorm to look for a ring for your mom. So off to the pawnshops we went. At the first pawnshop there was a magnificent opal ring – your mom's favorite – surrounded by a cover of little diamonds. I could not resist. It cost a whopping $250.00 but it was worth every penny of it. It was cute to see her. She felt so guilty for having so much spent on her. Typical mothers, she is always ready to give and serve, but when the same is done to her she slinks back in abundant sacrificial anguish. Finally, she blurts out, "It's nice, I like it". Only the inner heart and the reader of this memo will know that it really isn't a several hundred dollar ring. Does it matter then to the bearer of the blue and red opal?

Yes! Kids, it's been quite some time since we flew together, one trip to the Caribbean, my two-week imbibing. It's one of those little opulent luxuries of the leisure class your family has not been able to afford. When I travel, by car, or by foot, I always have you in mind and in touch, often by phone.

Now during the rest of my life, I don't know how much we will travel together.

Be assured; however, whenever I go you will be with me always, I don't need to say that much of my life has centered around you - my children. With you I wouldn't have traveled anywhere; without you I wouldn't have seen anything; without you I certainly wouldn't have had a meaning for my existence. Whatever else has happened, thank you for these things and...

"Are you ready to go?"

Let's fly together.

Dad

Dear Kids,

Re: "Save for a Rainy Day and Retirement"

One pursues a job (career) for a variety of reasons. One is if you don't work you don't eat – we will accept the thousands who are on welfare. At least any self-respecting person works to achieve the basic necessities of life and then some.

The "then some" is what makes the difference between a humdrum existence, meager survival, and a life catapulted to some degree of comfort. This cannot come about except when:

> You get into an occupation which brings security.
> You get into a pattern of saving and investing.
> You enroll into a retirement program through your work or private insurance.

Five or ten percent of your income may seem needed when you begin your career,   buying a home, car and all. A slight sacrifice early will bring untold dividends later.

Now your mother and I are cases in point. For thirty years we have lived hand to mouth, payday to payday. Although a bad business venture, as a result of the loss of my job due to alcoholism, has set us back half a million dollars, our way has been to spend what you got on the table and wait until the next pay period. Now at the age of retirement we know this isn't the way to go.

Take my advice so you will be comfortable and secure long after we are gone. Sock a little away each day and month by month. Don't live an extravagantly blessed life till the end of your time!

Love,

Dad

Dear Kids,

Re: Kids, Stay Away From All Addictions, Even the Good Ones

Life presents many hurdles which we humans must jump. Some are easier than others. The more difficult ones are stopping a bad habit and starting an activity which is good for us. Let me illustrate. Since being diagnosed with diabetes, I have been advised over and over that exercise is necessary for proper healing. Fully knowing this, I can't motivate myself to get on with this. Help me with my inaptness.

But there is a much bigger problem, right here in "River City". That is the problem of investing something small for a much greater return. Take a chance! A chance on what, I say! Making it big – lotteries, you name it. Or play old blackjack down at the casino.

Now the reason I am concerned about these things has to do with the underlying principle involved. It's not the loss of money, though this is significant in its own right. What is the love of money, and the portentousness to gamble a little to make a lot which in the main means losing a lot? Too much in fact!

What is it about the gambling experience to make it dangerous? It's what some call the allure; others the grab. It seems that since the first moment that one easily comes out ahead a few dollars, the bite (grab) is made. Sometimes slowly, sometimes quickly, the iron claw of greed grabs hold of a person. No one can hardly define it nor explain its presence, but it is just as sure and steady as gravity itself. It is tenacious and progressive. It clenches until the very entrails of a person are exposed. When you're caught, you're caught and no human power can release you from its grasp.

I often wonder why some people surrender to the grasp and others do not. I have come to believe that it is a matter of psychology. The allure! The excitement! The adrenalin rush! All are part of a fantasy, which means not only to get something for nothing, but that you somehow are favored by the Gods and this is your destiny.

However, you are no different from another. You are a number on a dice. If you win - five others lose. And when you and your fellows lose, a small minority wins. Isn't this the way of capitalism? Think before you buy a ticket! Think before you play. It may no longer be recreation, it may be an escape valve for society, made up of frustrated people who don't really only not know right from wrong but who are caught up in a whirlwind of spiritual decadence.

Yours truly,

Dad

Dear Kids,

Re: On Joining or Becoming a Citizen.

By accident or parental planning, one is co-joined with the human race at birth, an event having great significance on the life of every being. The time in history and the place in geography are all important in the life of an individual. They will tell you your size and shape, what you wear on all occasions, your eating style and stuff, and virtually every attribute and habit which you will carry through life.

In still another way, we are catapulted into the diversion of citizenship. I am a bonafide Yankee, member of the United States - However, I am and I'm not. I was born in Colorado, raised in Idaho, and lived in a half-dozen other states. What does this mean? What does it mean to be an American? Well! I lived there for thirty years and still don't know.

Through a twist of fate, I have spent over thirty five years in a new country, Canada, in the Province of Alberta. That move came on July 14, 1969. In 1992, I applied for Canadian citizenship. That stuff is a paper.

What does it mean to join another country at the age of 54?

Try it and you will know!

Love,

Dad

Dear Kids,

Re: What to Do About Betrayal?

You gotta start somewhere. A tentative meaning will do. I am betrayed when others don't live up to my expectations (desires) for them. I betray others when I don't live up to their desires for me. I betray myself on two ways, when I don't fill the need to be the person I want to be or become the person I think others expect of me..

I can do a lot of preaching to you about being true and honorable to others and being of utmost true to oneself. Any amount of preaching can never replace one fundamental tenet. You can never be true to yourself if you are not true to your brother and sister.

What are these elements of virtue which come out all the way from a white lie to the invasion of someone by taking their life? It is written - "Thou shalt not steal", "Thou shalt not lie", "Thou shalt not kill". Now I tell you more than this. "Thou shalt not betray thyself to self. But the greatest commandment of all, "Do not betray yourself to others". You can only do this if you are true to yourself.

The test of life is truth. The test of truth is honor to others. Do not abscond with the privacy or personal values of others; at the same time never surrender your own values and retain your right to privacy although you should freely surrender it when a fellow human cries for help.

The quality of your life will never be measured by the esteem which you command from others; living attains merit only when you share your experience with another human being.

A virtuous life is one shared accurately and honestly. Neither stands above the other. People differ in their experience. And some experiences are more honorable than others. But by relating exactly what the experience is, I can make a clear choice of its value to me. Then betrayed is out of the question.

Yours sincerely,

Dad

P.S. Be your honest self. Don't deceive.

Dear Kids,

Re: Remember the Good Old Days!

Have you ever heard your father say, "You don't know what it was like when I was a kid"? Well! I'm the dad. I told you of this. My father told me of it. My Granddad told my father.

Those were the days of the model T. Working from sunup to sundown, those days were when air-conditioned combines were not even dreamed of. Families were large and living details were intricate and delicate. It was another time, a different era. So what was so good about the good old days? It's not that I search for, or yearn for, today to be an exact replica of the past. But I yearn for some of those principles for which they stood. What I remember I love today.

Yet there is a more important reason to revere the past. What I am today is what I once was. What I was, was an instrument of the times and conditions in which I lived. I am what I was and have become, yet the present offers more than mere fascination. Today, I can choose not to live in the yesterday, in its misery or glory. Today I am captured with an obsession. I can be whatever I want to be. I have a choice. The world is mine to make in my own image. It will be to my liking because I shape it myself. This I don't depend on yesterday for a guide to today.

So yesterday, today, and tomorrow seemingly make up the essence of time. I think there is another alternative, one of great value when one forgets time. That is the uncontested moment of the present. The moment reveals two elements of reality – the inner and outer. The inner means those things which pertain to self and its workings. The outer refers to those other than self phenomenon. No other realm can exist.

Knowing just exactly what I think and feel is all that I really possess. When I own it and I know that it's mine, I can effectively give it away or modify it as I see fit. Thus the moment consists not only how I think and feel, but how I present these commodities for the world to see.

The great problem in today's world is that the great bulk of people present to the world such a pyramid of images that hardly anyone can recognize who they are, and if they recognize them at one moment, they may appear different at the next moment. Before I die, I will try to present to you the way I really am in a consistent and straight-forward way.

Trying to be real, moment by moment

Dad

Dear Kids,

Re: "Cure Your Soul"

Imagine you have an obtrusive genie inside you that responds when you say "I want to be happy", or "I am going to be sad". You may, indeed, command this genie for whatever task you wish.

The most fundamental task of the modern era is caring for the soul. Without proper care, soul deprivation leads to the most devastating body and mind confusions of all time. Among the poignant symptoms are emptiness, meaninglessness, depression, disillusionment, loss of values, yearnings for personal fulfillment, and a hunger for spirituality.

Kids, "I don't want you to be plagued by this modern day pandemic – soullessness. Tend to yourself, your spirit, and its need for religion. The task – your lifetime chore – is soul reconciliation. Symptomology cannot be abated by conquering the material world; you must deal with the mystical spirit. Take care of that vague essence – your soul.

Here's what you might try.

Let go of the "Tasmanian devil" within. Open your heart to confess that barbaric little soul breaker. Every person has buried within days events that truly haven't been. Admit these to someone in a humbly honest way, and your total biological and spiritual systems will respond with a sense of healthy freedom even the experts can't explain.

If you don't talk out your imminent secrets then, write them down. A similar kind of cleaning effect will occur; they depend on your need for it.

If you are inhibited from talking it out, another useful tool is to write about it. Include the facts of your experience along with your feelings about the events. Select a period of time, no more than 30 minutes, in a private place where you don't want to be interrupted.

Can one know what is true anymore; or if it is not true? The answer must come from you. Try it and see if it fits. If it feels good, it will tend to your soul. Not to heal everything, but it will help to elevate your spiritual condition.

You may not wish to write daily, but writing about the traumas in your life can help integrate these into your experience. Morbid as it may seem, when I die, or mom dies, find a quiet place of resolve and explore your most intimate feelings about it. I did this when my dad died, although I spoke into a tape recorder intermittently from Lethbridge to New Plymouth, Idaho. It's nothing for publication; it sure dealt with a variety of feelings.

Write or talk to a confidante. You will be surprised at the results. Through this may your journey be swift and your voyage easier.

Love and God Bless!
Dad

Dear Kids,

Re: "Learning Not to Use Put Downs"

Before talking about their use, I want to explore the synonyms for put downs. A strategist might say "the only way you can relate to others, by putting them down just to boost your own ego" (J.J. Dec. 25/92) another version of this classic ego enhancer is when an individual denigrates another without their presence for the purpose of gaining superiority over them.

A neutral and less offensive degrader is overt and covert criticism usually culminating in judgment. Any statement devaluing character or performance "less than" needed desired, or expected by the speaker is degrading and mortifying. Many of these subterranean excursions utilize built-in equipment for devaluation - cultural labels and stereotypes. It is self devaluation and personal degradation with which I am concerned. Most of these are probably in the form of jokes; but whatever literary form it takes, the reciprocal is always someone feeling less about oneself.

Sitting here on Christmas Day, 1992, in Grandmas and Grandpa's living room, I just developed the framework for a new game. The one who observes the most put downs wins. Each time anyone perceives another putting another down, the perpetrator owes the observer a dollar.

Now that put downs have been defined, it is important to distinguish why they are launched, sometimes innocently, but most often viciously with intent.

What is a joke or light humor at another's expense? I am not advocating this common ego genocide. Other opportunity prevails if only we take action.

Instead of bringing the ego crumbling down with our verbal onslaughts, why not use the same tool to elevate another person. Catapult them to their own dimension by using the creative forces to buoy them up.

When you are fully comfortable with the game of affirmation, try it on non-family members; try it on your favorite waitress at your coffee hangout. Try it on your minister. Dig into every crack and crevice you can find, **AFFIRM SOMEONE**. Do it even when it seems hard to do.

The most effective opposition to a put down is a gentle smile. It is contagious and eternal. Lots of opportunities prevail. Act on them rather than dormant being reactive.

My family! My family! I adore you. Please don't put me down.

Dad

Dear Kids,

Re: "Honesty is The Best Policy"

When I was a little boy in New Plymouth, I had the urge to take a 1 cent piece of bubble gum from a shelf at the service station where I was later to work as a gas pump jockey. Cagily picking it up, I cautiously unwrapped the gum and started its approach to my mouth. Then, suddenly, as if my hand became paralyzed, I realized just exactly what I was doing. I carefully dropped the gum in a convenient hiding place behind the pop cooler. I felt relieved. I had caught myself before I became a thief.

Some years later another test of my honesty presented itself at the same place. I overcharged a tourist something like $1.00 for the gas he had purchased. So alarmed at such a hint of dishonesty, I jumped in dad's truck, chased the car several miles down the road leaving the station unattended; flagged the tourist down and made the proper change.

Somewhere between the art of stealing and righting dishonest mistakes, lies a whole spectrum of doubtful integrity and cast iron verbosity. Almost all of us swing back and forth on this pendulum. One who has thoroughly tested the waters does not hesitate to say "Honesty is the best policy".

How is this translated into action in all of our practical affairs? The answer is not simple for in every circumstance there is a judge. When you are the judge, calls can't always be based on theodicy. There must be room for error - - human error. To err is human. The separation of you from your neighbor is a form of humanness.

No one can accurately take stock of all their human errors. It is more important, however, to recognize our human propensity to err. When we give ourselves permission to make a mistake of honesty; we may not be so daring to try and get away with dishonesty the next time.

Society can only be a just and honest place if the individuals who make it up pursue these virtues. Thus, anytime any members cheats, steals, or lies, the foundation is eroded a little. Each person counts. If one person does pick away at our foundation, a dozen or so others will be affected. The resulting effect snowballs. As injustice may sometimes prevail, the ultimate good coming from the greatest number believing and acting on it will produce the greatest of all possible worlds. Not a perfect world by any means; but the best we may always strive for. Stand up and be counted! Be honest!

Dad

Dear Kids,

Re: On Finding Meaning

Live as you will, but somehow pass through the eye of the needle to find something very meaningful in your life.

Meaning surrounded you from the time you were wished for until this very day. And I am urging you to develop an aura of meaning that will surround you for the rest of your life.

We hurled demonstrations of meaning at you since birth. We bombarded you with our configurations until you left home, and then came back again. We have tried to tell you in word, deed, and things what to search for in this life.

Not exactly knowing if we were too early, or too late, or even right, our legacy is now your own. You are obligated to choose the style of your life and give it that meaning which will propel you to heights of ecstasy, or to the depths of despair.

What will you do? What will you – find meaningful in your life? The arts? Classics? A touch of musical verbosity? A vintage wine? No. I am not suggesting the usual preoccupation with cultural symbols. The search is much deeper than this. It seeks the components of the soul and the food that feeds it. My advice is, "Take care of your soul". Anything that nurtures the spirit is meaningful, whatever tarnishes it, evil.

What is the elusive part of our essence euphemistically called the soul. I think the most characteristic is the element of genuineness. It also has depth. Your soul is also singular. No one can tell you how to live your life. So you must take care of your own soul.

You must become a tradesman to care for your soul, to "craft your life". An artisan of unquestionable merit, the rewards come from looking at the stars for extraordinary revelation. The mystical answer will leave you with one extraordinary fact. Only you can reflect and answer on the way your life has taken shape.

If you tend to the soul as Nathaniel Hawthorne mused on finding happiness. "Happiness is like the butterfly. When you chase it, it eludes you. But when you seek appropriate matters of concern, it sets gently on your shoulder."

Search for food for the hungry heart is similar. Soul nurture is a byproduct of living life to the best of your ability exercising the principles of good living. Then shall the fruits of the spirit will be abundantly forthcoming to you.

The concern is not where you have traveled on the sea of life, or the ports of call, but what your destination is from your last point of departure. Meaning is the justification for directing your soul. It's like a direction finder; it alerts you to your destination. Noting the scenes and landmarks approached and passed along the way, you will be in a position to declare on the last day, "It was a beautiful journey". Stop only at those ports of call for something which you need; not what you wish for!

Have a good journey,

Dad

Dear Kids,

Re: **Integration:** Both Moral and Societal

I want to share with you some of my feelings about interdependence and family integration. In a sense, cohesiveness and interdependence are intertwined. I feel close to you and have always felt there has been a honey like substance causing us to stick together. Some of the stickiness is caused by pain when the two of you were young and had multiple stops in the hospital. Watching someone you love suffer makes you appreciate their real value to you. Thus, year after year, you grew dearer to me through our mutual pain – you the recipient and me the observer.

Then, when you were mere babes you became the observer of our family illness - the abuse of alcohol; therein started a progression of a family banned by synergy to one bound by toxins. The absence of father and the absence of quality time with me surely imprinted the psyche and soul of you, my children.

There was a kicker that helped save the day, at least for Jeff and perhaps as for you, Jenni. Crises brought us close. When as parents we were required to deal with the potential of your death – you're not breathing and lost to consciousness - - we quickly and forever more had the value of you to dance before our very eyes. We wanted your presence with us.

Those traumatic moments of not-so-quiet desperation made your mom and I realize a fundamental principle of life. It is only in the throes of losing something that you really assess and value that something by knowing how much it means to you.

It is not only apparent that one's choice possessions generate an insatiable attraction for its owner, the owner about to lose something he cherishes learns an immense lesson. It equips them to value and cherish what others hold dearly.

Now as someone who has seen ample pain and destruction, I solemnly declare now, that your pain was my pain. I am also proud to admit that another's pain became my own. I would carry you across the threshold of despair. In the event I need to share some pain with you - please carry my load. Then, and only then, we are part of a common destiny.

Let's heal together,
Dad

Dear Kids:

Re: When Driving, Don't Pick up Strays!

In the journey of life, whatever your station may be, your encounters result in crossing the paths of many others. Some of those will be highly respected people. There are numerous others you will encounter, however, that are of questionable character. Theirs is a world of alcohol, drugs, or what have you. A world made up of escapism. They are the strays, the rage of society, the dispossessed and uncared for. They are the ones my mother warned me about. However, she didn't tell me that their heinous acts can be directed to you as well as the next guy.

Those soul parched people who have fallen through the cracks are from every race and creed. Located from sea to shining sea, they exist in any city, Canada. Colorful words do not tell the story of their hearts. These are written on the wind whose beginnings or endings no one really knows and most don't care about.

Life, as generous in all ways that it is, divulges to both the needy and well kempt its plentiful gifts of wares. Among the requirements are the hurt and brokenhearted. You kids call them strays and even though I sometimes call them misfits, I know who they really are. They are the person next door, the one down the street and across town – they are the strays I identify with. Why? Because I am one of them! As one of them, the law of gravity and depravity operate. People, like cream, rise to their own level. My level is not where the action is, it's where the hurt is. That's why I'm down there with my people grubbing.

Now kids! Here's the kicker. Some of these strays I pick up are horse thieves and culprits. They not only steal from their grandmother but also from me and my family. So when our dog sitter scoffed $5,000 worth of our family possessions over a past Christmas holiday, you might say, "trust", "trust who?" My answer," Only those whom you know absolutely to be honest". Be they one or the other, I must adhere to the principle of my grandmother or anyone's grandmother. It' the grandma principle - "Treat everyone as though they are your friend".

Trust everyone or trust no one. My alternatives are limited. I guess I'll opt for the former and suffer the deprivation and cost of being empty pocketed and humiliated on many occasions.

Any sage advice suggests that your own targets of trust may be culpable. They might defile one's prerogative of making their own inept judgments of others actual virtues. So as you travel through life look at your fellows and say, "you're worth my trust", or "my trust is greater than you". Whatever, be prepared to accept the consequences.

Love,
Dad

Dear Kids,

Re: Wanna take Boz for a Walk?

This is not a rhetorical question. It is, however, opening the door of a paradox! For half of our dog's life, I thought it was a burdensome chore to go out and walk the dog around the neighborhood. You must have thought so too, because of your denying what could be an invigorating past time of yester year. I know you haven't been up to doing the duty of giving Boz his exercise lately. Heed my invitation from the new born Dad; the walk of the past with the walk of today offers new and absolutely spectacular opportunities.

I discovered that walking makes you feel better. I should have taken a cue from Boz a long time ago that doing something which is naturally good for you is fun to do. When you ask him, "Are you ready?" his answer is apparent as his jumping, reactive behavior which only blindness could miss. He not only gets excited when he is invited for his daily walk, the exuberance he portrays throughout the journey can only lead to one inimical conclusion – animals have an instinct for knowing what is good for them.

The appreciation of Boz's enthusiasm is shadowed by the benefits to the benevolent master. He who walks the dog has access to any, or all of, the following:

1. The hues and color of the sky, in sunshine and rain, provides a myriad of colors that the creative mind could not envision. Surely the great painter of the sky has an endless reservoir of beauty just waiting to be seen by the appreciated audience of Boz and master. The artist's talent is not the only dividend for a giver to Boz.

2. Hear the breeze or wind, whatever the day happens to bring, reminds me of the old biblical question, "Where does the wind begin" and "Where does it all end?" The stream of creation raises a similar conundrum.

Yet floating gently in the sky beckoning to the other elements is that gentle and tantalizing breeze.

Envision the ducks and geese with their distinctive and particularistic call. In pairs or groups they seem to cover the lake in which they swim.

The moon, on a late night walk, glistens with a brilliant reflection on the water. Couple this with the aroma of freshly scented air, as though the raindrops leave a fragrance as they pass through it.

The walks of today are indeed, different than those of yesterday. Add all the elements, too numerous to mention, together and you have a bountiful world of beauty coming to you. There is another thought relating to nature and your loveable dog. When you take this walk with someone you deeply love, it simply cannot be equaled. This is one way your mom and I have developed closeness lately. So is it any wonder that when it gets that time of day to take Boz, I become fidgety, too. One other thing before we start today's walk. Boz has spirit and his quick wit prompts him to tug nervously at his leash. He seems to say, "Let me go as fast as I can". But when you say, "Slow down, Boz" you are giving yourself a good cue! As you pace yourself; you pace your dog. When your dog paces you, synchronicity is created! The end result is that the fast moving world of the day becomes manageable. I usually take two deep breaths on each walk and find that my heart slows down. I slow down and live awhile - - at least 25 minutes walking the dog.

How about it? Do you want to take Boz for a walk?

Love,

Dad

Dear Kids,

Re: On Controlling

Using my own powers to alter the conditions of people, places and things of my environment is the best gift God has given me. When I use that gift to promote things exclusively for me, a rather evil shadow surrounds me.

Where does the delicate balance lie between my own interests and those of my fellows? This is probably one of the more salient conundrums of all time. Its scope, being beyond my control, leaves me as a reactor and heavily co-dependent.

Controlling is using the power of your person and techniques of persuasion to influence the outcome of your own, or another's life's chances. They may come from personal and legitimized power. Power runs away when it contravenes natural justice. Hiring a female or minority to fill an institutional quota is not justice; it is a place to create natural disturbances. The same for a black minority; it adds an insult to justice.

Dad;

one of many

Dear Son:

Re: Pass it on to Ty and Explain it to Him

This letter is especially for you. It is especially painful for me to write. I must tell you from the bottom of my heart what's been going through my mind in these last torturous hours.

I know now that you will never be what I wanted you to be. You have given me much more than what I wanted. It wasn't merchant, or chief, I wanted. I was gracious enough to bet you would be a doctor (medical that is), or lawyer. You have given me a chance to have my parenthood.

Discovering your grades were not up to snuff for you obtaining the professions I chose for you, I now have to deal with the paltry 2.4 grade point average in pursuit of a B.S. degree in Psychology, is this all there is to it? Must I now love the near son in an unconditional way? Must I accept him for less than my hopes and desires?

I answer emphatically to you my son, my one and only son, that it's not that I must accept you. I cherish the opportunity and thank God that I have the rest of my life to know you for what you are and what you have become.

Let's leave this for a moment while I try to tell you the importance of achieving these much revered positions. Let it be known at the very outset it's not the respect. I harbor for the tasks noble professions do.

As it were, I hold much contempt for the myths surrounding the better occupations. Society seems to think that those who get there, is so through hard work and initiative. Such nonsense! Then to make matters whose the higher professions tend to be treated with such awe as the tendered respect might make them sacred. It's not all that stuff I wanted for you son. Leaving my penchant toward vanity behind, I seek for you to have life easy enough to be enjoyed. Someone might say, "Don't give me that bull; you just want your kid to be important".

That's part of it, maybe, but the big picture embraces more than a mere image model of life.

If you ask me, "What will I do when I grow up, Dad?" My answer will be, "Choose something you believe in with all your heart, mind and soul". Then, pursue it with everything that's in you and then some. This same is the plus element, that energy of the universe available to all, all those who believe. Believe in yourself, son. The world will be your most severe taskmaster. Take the lessons it gives you, calculate your course based on these lessons and trod to the control of your destiny. It's all up to you. Drive your own bus to the journeys end.

Love,
Dad

Dear Kids,

Re: What to do When you Miss the Train

I assume in this short discourse that the train is the fastest and easiest way to your destination, gives a need you sense to go somewhere. Remember, if you don't know where you're going you will wind up somewhere else!

Let's do a little inventory taking so when all the cards are on the table and all things being equal, you or I can decidedly and precisely make a determination as to when to go and what arrangements to make.

Somewhere from earth I have to determine if I wish to go to the old worst world or the new world. To determine this, I must know where I am to begin. Am I in the old and want to get to the new or in the new and want to get to the old. Do I simply want to stay in my present world? I guess I'll stay in my own world and take the train to somewhere.

I have wondered often how far it is from half-way from nowhere to somewhere. Is it like getting an unlimited pass on the train to ride anywhere whenever I so desire. This plan would be folly amenable to the machinations of going without direction.

Not so! In my life I want to have a picture of where I'm going and how to get there. I guess I'll take the train. Is there really somewhere to go? What if the real world tells me I have nowhere to go? So I have learned to use map quest.

Happy traveling,

Dad

Dear Kids,

Re: Walking the Tread Mill of Life

I don't believe eternity can ever be experienced in an hour. I retract from numerous experiences and share only the possibilities of slow plodding time as it counts its way toward my death. Before that fatality occurs, I wish to share more with you about that treadmill of life which brings us to this formidable state not of our own accord; it will also take over against our wishes.

Between these extremes of birth and death, what meaning can we glean from the interface of coming and going? Living death from most of this lifetime only prepares me for the incontrovertible conclusion. If there is any meaning in life, it is that luminous sphere which engulfs you when you are thoroughly convinced life has a meaning. Your meaning is concocted by you and used as an agent of transformation between the childish instincts and the adult ego; meaning propels you through life.

Where you are at each moment is a definition of life. Depression and ecstasy, joy and sorrow, happiness and sadness are not only part of each moment; they are part of the moment which are part of eternity. It's not the task of tomorrow that makes life, it's the present moment. Success should not be measured by accomplishments; it should be measured by how you feel about life.

My dear children, I became a bastion of spiritual sickness when I desired you to climb the status ladder. I didn't realize my error until you were adults and chose what you wanted for your lives, which direction you should to go. Forgive me, please, for wanting you to be someone I wanted you to be. Forgive me for not wanting you to be you.

Today I feel that my discomfort stems from unresolved issues in me. I feel akin to ferocity of a caged animal struggling to find its own freedom. I picture a coyote walking back and forth in his cage looking for an escape door. The real "I" am behind a locked door. It can't always be a glass door with a glass window for others to peer through and find what is behind the door. These are prisons and insane asylums.

Words cannot describe what is there, but a resurrected dad may appear. Who that will be, nobody knows...not even God.

As for you, always be honest and open to yourselves and to the world. You will be who you want to be and the world will be at your command. The divine will flow through you in such measure you will be equal to the angels. Believe in yourselves, my children, but also believe from whence you came and where you are to go.

The dark nights of the soul will be known for what they are, and your encounter with the divine will be what sets you free. You will be loosened from the tie that binds and your new freedom will be the pinnacle of your life. You will see yourselves anew, and the world, too.

Remember after midnight comes the darkness of pre-dawn. And then the sunlight will shine through – through you and the world.

I love you unconditionally,

Dad

Dear Kids,

Re: The Wrong Model

Most all of your growing years, difficulties existed between us due to a large part that I did not take the role of being a parent. Being a parent put me into a role I really didn't know how to play out. To make yours a better world and one which would bring you imminent success, I thought you should live up to my expectations. You should have chores to do and do them according to my time schedule. Your friends should pass my approval. The how and why of your school performances must reflect the standards of my liking. To capsule it all very succinctly, your mother and I were really trying to clone you. But Aha! It didn't work.

The model was wrong. My paradigm didn't change until after you had grown up, so, I'd like to present it to you now hoping beyond hope, that if you have children sometimes you may use my experience as a lesson to go by.

You must first remember your children are unique individuals. They should have certain rights and privileges. Among these are the rights to pursue happiness and the right to act responsibly on their own terms and not you the parents. It is not necessary to clone yourself through your children. It is important to you as parent to lower your expectations of your children.

Everyone grows and develops at their individual pace. Sometimes they spurt and grow quickly; at other times it seems like they will never grow up. Different levels of growth are also seen in your children if you will just let them be themselves and honor their own individuality.

They shouldn't have to do chores at an exact time because the parent thinks it's the right time. Every child will accept their own responsibility if given the opportunity. The individuality of each child is seen only through that child and not through comparisons to others.

Love

Dad

Dear Kids,

Re: Listen to the Wisdom of your Kids

God is our father; we are his children. This is no less for a fourteen year old than a sixty year old. Being a parent doesn't give us a right to be a dictator. Let us all pursue the democratic way. May we listen to each other, not only to words spoken, but to that which isn't said?

Our children have an untold world of experience in their hearts. They are people, too. Let's listen to them. Kids, I wish I had listened to you!

Love,

Dad

Dear Kids,

Re: Finalizing my Concerns to You

These notes I write to you finalize the concerns I have about you. I can only separate myself from you in this world and the world to come by declaring my independence from you.

To be independent does not replace my caring. Most important is my desire and commit-mint to love you unconditionally. A most difficult task, it has not always been easy to do this.

How can a father not want or even expect great things to happen to and for his children. Woe to me to let by gone days not permit me to worry about your education, your careers, whether you can buy a home or not and a myriad of other concerns which beguile one in daily living. Are there moments when thoughts of death, threatening sickness do not take its toll on the inner heart of a father?

You see! When children about die in this life with the parent standing by their side unable to do anything; one learns to value the precious nature of life. I have loved you in sickness and in health. Now as to death I must part, I wonder what you will do with your memories of this life.

I know my journey through alcoholism will be quick to appear, especially for Jenni and Jeff. The lost times, the ball games, playing catch with dad, going for an evening walk, building castles in the sand–these and many more are the could-have-beens if alcohol had not absorbed my attention while you were young.

Then in your teen years–with the turmoil you went through–I was in a recovery stage and unable to always be there for you. But now you are all adults. To help you along the way, I give one final word of advice. In life, live to the fullest and, above all, don't commit the same faults as your parents. God knows, I tried this and failed. This is for the four of you, my biological kids Jenni and Jeff, and the adopted kids, Julie and Jennifer.

Love
Dad

Dear Kids,

Re: On Labels

As you wander through life, you are going to cross paths will many people who will label you such as doctors and teachers, parents or friends and so on. They may say you have the dreaded bi-polar disorder of manic depression or they may make statements about personality disorders. They may say you should be in the *sparrow group* at school instead of *the robins*. The labels which will be assigned to you will be almost without number.

The only way to life in a world of being labeled is to know you well enough so that the labels have little impact. Don't let the labels fit. They are only stickers to peel off and cast aside on the junk pile of life.

What is left when labels are discarded is the real you. You will be so authentic to yourself, so ultimately comfortable in your own skin that your humanness shines above all else. But there will be those times; times of unbearable anguish you must endure. At these times you may need labels to help you through. But don't take them that seriously.

May I suggest you put them in the junk pile and replace them with your own ecstasy?

Your dad, who has been there.

Love

Dear Kids,

Re: Searching for a Purpose in life

Life's twists and turns never end until you die. There is no guarantee that this is the end of it all. All of us are here for a short time and for many of us it is not a good time.

As I sit here in this slum pub tonight, I have the strongest desire for tears to stream down my face– they just won't come. I am numb from trying to answer the question, "What is the purpose of life?" and "What is God's will for my life?"

Was I saved from perilous death through drunkenness to have a life so emotionally down; a spark of life is a faint echo of long, lost dreams. How many years did I stroll the streets of Las Vegas, Corvallis, Tacoma, Columbia, and Jefferson City looking for a ray of sunshine in my life? How many times did life pass me by after I was destroyed from alcoholism, only to find out about supercilious wonder which smothered me? I was a pilgrim with no emotional home.

As my soul has wandered listlessly through the universe in a random way for many years; when I die please cast my ashes to the wind. I will be happy to know that one speck of my dust might fall at the roots of a solid oak tree, another by a leaf to dance blissfully as it waves through eternity. Another might float to earthen waters to look and drink to an ocean clear or a delta of stars new shining.

Let my remains fly high and furiously for in this life the fury I lived had no recompense to secure me a desire fulfilled - a subtle spot on this planet. As I dance to the tune of no drummer, I died to the sound of hollowness on the earth. As I searched for love, loneliness flowed from closed ears.

I make my final sacrifice to life. I tried to help Shari love life, but I lost my life in trying to give it. Alas! You reap what you sew. But I have nowhere to lay my head, and nothing more to give. At 59 years old when I wrote this and now at 71 years, I am old beyond my years. I have given till I'm empty and there's nothing or no one to fill my cup. My cup runneth over because I HAVE YOU AND and I have MY GRANDCHILDREN.

DAD

Dear Kids,

Re: Asking Life to Deliver you From its Bondage

My soul lies barren in the desolation of my own trap. Its jaws too powerful for me to release, I writhe in agony as the drum continues to play. I ask life to deliver me from its bondage. Just as I was thrown into this world, I hope that fate will throw me out of this world.

Burn me to ashes! Can matter be either created or destroyed? What matters in this world of soul are the words I have built my life on? Are they ethereal nothingness to mix with no less than the day's dung?

If God is the partner of my most intimate soliloquies let me sit at the top of the balance rock on monumental creek, or stand before the ghosts of yester years to resonate lectures to hundreds of students in those hallowed rooms. Where and how did the dragon of life close the gate to the path of holiness to find me the brunt of mental illness and alcoholism?

Beware – Oh ye who seek worldly wisdom; life will soon speed by you as an overburdened locomotive and it will as a final gesture to your eternal flame–the fire which sends your skin to burnt ashes. "Whetted shall I do with his remains?"

I don't know. Let him fly away home.

Dear Kids,

Re: Do you Have a Real Father?

I must ask the question now on the eve of asking my children to leave my house. I would call these people I love. Have they ever accepted me as father? They may be good reasons for this.

In these memoirs to my kids, I had hoped to give them what I most value in my life–me and the values I cherish. Having brought two kids into the world and seeing them raised in my presence under the guise of alcoholism, I now must openly admit to them and to any of the world who cares that alcohol makes a dismal failure of fathers.

Drinking before and after they were born and until the eldest was 15 and the younger 13, I drank the years of parenting away. My children grew up with my expectations that they were unable to live up to. My severe criticisms of their efforts left them with very deep; impenetrable resentment which I doubt can ever be totally healed.

When one is paralyzed by alcohol, it is impossible to know the deep wounds which are created in relationships. Such was the case for my children, especially my younger one, Jeff. When I followed the program of recovery, I tried to make an amends to him about the disastrous father/son relationship that was so strained. His response was "It happened so let's forget about it and get on with life". I now realize he didn't then and even now realize he can't so easily forget.

Now as a final note, I wish to offer some advice. If you ever have children, and I sincerely hope that you do, please try to be a father to them because it is very, very painful to admit that you missed the boat because you could have been a father and wasn't good enough in your own eyes.. Don't let the opportunity be muffled.

Love,

Dad

Dear Kids,

Re: Underlining a Message of Hope

I want to accentuate the possible and not depreciate the probable. Hope, in a world which is suffocating, would hardly raise the spirits of me an estranged victim. That is how I view my life; it needs to be surviving brother of a dying civilization which had lead its bronchial tubes shut off.

The life saving adrenalin gives a rush of unquenchable relief. Life continued. That is the hidden message underlying all hope. The very essence of life has thrown me into a bottomless pit. When I am temporarily caught on a cleft, soon the downward spiral plunges me further into the black abyss till finally no light can be seen in any direction.

This is the time succulent hope must raise its sweet head. From beneath all mire lies the Phoenix of life.

I have searched all earthen vessels and have come up empty. More must be after three score and ten years. Mutual funds have a pay off, but the search goes deeper than tinker tape.

I am beyond Screw Type Letters; the diagnosis is spiritual deprivation with delirium tremors. My ego is calling for help; it lies within. Alas! I am told to have hope.

The seeds were sewn for hope some twenty five years ago. I thought alcohol to be the problem. After more than meetings of A.A to many to count, I failed to find the answer there. Instead, I found hundreds of craving people unwilling to admit the true nature of the malady–a soul sickness. Now that I have the diagnosis, how do I heal this sickness in my life?

Again I have hope. Hope is anticipating a future state of affairs than what exists today. I am not sure how much of the present need to be exposed to give this morning, I don't think the kind of hope needing to be will evolve from pure humanism. The very best of any man's accomplishment cannot fill the hunger of my soul. I could be the richest man in Babylon and not be happy.

I must go to the source and find hope for my eternal being. My second career was a rag picker and the sickness of human souls was so rotten that the cancer of spirit found a home in my own spirit. I was left not wanton of neglect, but starved of the very stuff which fulfills the soul. The earth's valley may seem like to the top of the mountain.

Letting the future aside, there may be hope for the eternal. Eschewing the past, nodding to the future, the present moment may be all that exists. Yet, questions about eternity create a world of conundrums. Even to ask for hope for my soul casts darkness upon the light. Is there no hope?

I know hope does not come from this world. The universal elixir has not quenched my thirst; rather it sabotaged the light emitting from what seemed eternal darkness. The seeds of hope, then, must stem from another world, the world of the light.

Hope is the belief I assent. It lies ahead of the now. Death gives me hope to "Is that all there is?" An unfilled life gives hope for tomorrow's gift of grace. I look for hope in the world, to have peace and happiness for all who hunger and seek it. I sense the only hope for me and all of mankind is to love one another and be loved in return. There lies the solution to all man's ills.

Who in the army of all the people in the world do I stop by and love? Is it my wife, children, or numerous relatives left by the way as life has been lived out? The preacher who eloquently professes as I sit quietly listening to his exhortation; the cashier who impatiently waits to attend me as I am rushed quickly through the pay line or a thousand other faces which silently pass in the night or the one who offers a moment's pleasure for a meager fee of a few dollars. All of these are to love and so many more.

Perhaps hope is loving the unlovable, including myself. The last gasp of a dying man may be to look despairingly at the moon and say, "I believe".

Yes, I believe there is hope for hunger, for the poor, for the insanity of wars, for the loneliness of a dying AIDS victim, for the illiteracy of them all.

I believe there's hope for them all because there is hope for me. It has bees said "whatever is done to the least of these is also done to me. I don't know what scenes will be told from the script of my life, but somehow, in ways not definable to me, there is hope. I lend this letter to two people - two A.A. friends who gave me hope at a low time in my life. It is entitled, Don't Quit.

The other one who died foolishly chasing his cap under an eighteen wheeler...

Dear Kids,

Re: On Relationships

Realizing that everyone must leave their own footsteps in the sand, I'd like to write you about relationships, those which are intimate and those which are not because this is where footsteps are made. The purpose of relationships may vary somewhat according to their nature, but all of them serve to satisfy basic human needs.

A key, perhaps the most important one, is openness and honesty. These are foundation elements for any good relationship. What happens when these are absent, it's like a cornerstone being moved from the foundation.

Personalities come and personalities go, but the lasting impact of a person is their opening the door to their inner selves as a light to others in seeing them as they are. An illumined soul, however fractured it may be, is more soothing than one hiding in the shadows.

Honesty doesn't shed one from all their problems. If one recognized the perils a ship rollicking in the storm may stay afloat if one honestly fixes the leaky frame. It's not that problems always have to be solved; looking seriously at them provides some redemption. Person-to-person-soul talk cannot heal at the human level. It is not necessary for everyone in life to believe in a transcendental; however, it pays to believe that some kind of integrating principle exists in this universe. There are a thousand billion stars in our galaxy and with a hundred billion–give or take a billion or two–stars in the universe. We may open ourselves to a spirit which belies the compartmentalizing of our little lives.

We come from nothing and perhaps go to nothing. If we understand the core of life to be revolving around the center of our being, our being is ourselves with one or more others revolving around it, this temporary state of affairs we find ourselves in is fulfilled when we are genuine selves.

"Be your honest self"

P.S. We may marry, divorce, go to war, and become engrossed in paying taxes, with enormous problems entering our lives but taking off our masks by being ourselves brings untold rewards. Just be yourself and you will one day be told, "Thanks for being exactly who you are".

Dad

Dear Kids,

Re: On Being Healthy

One of my greatest heartfelt needs is for you to be healthy. Thus, it may be helpful to tell you what I mean by this. It is common these days of this speaking of physical, mental, spiritual and emotional health. I like to combine these in one reference to health. Scott Peck's words fit here, "An illness or disease is any defect in the structure of our bodies or personalities that prevents us from fulfilling our potential as human beings". .

With interpretation this could fit anywhere we might apply it. To heal is to make whole or sound–free from ailment. To get well, to bring about a cure in the individual is one ideal. There is another meaning, healing trouble among people; to bring to an end to conflicts between people. There is a way to restore former amity between individuals.

The process of gaining individual and collective health in simple terms is overcoming sin. Sin is any departure from perfection. It manifests in illness and disease. There are, of course, different levels of cures through the basics of love. Love is the antidote for individual disease and social strife. This can be found in untold resources of books. It is beyond my capability to argue the merits of love in action. Its healing power is beyond reproach and stands undaunted as personal growth potential. This is the beginning and end. My desire for you is to have love from which you have health. Although the great equation is love; sometimes health chinks enter in. The greater your love is, the better your health. Over the long haul this is a cosmic law and the percentages are on your side.

Dad

Dear Kids,

Money Matters

I would like to leave you some advice on money matters–before I die. The first law of life is, "He who doesn't work, doesn't eat". I am not referring to the pilferers of the system who are parasites. I am not a conservative, but I have come to know many are capable of giving back to society, but willfully choose not to.

The next law is to pay yourself from what you earn. Your mother and I have spent our whole working life living from paycheck to paycheck, without saving a snitch. How much you pay yourself is variable, but a good guideline is one-tenth of your earnings.

I also urge you to invest wisely. To do this, go to the financial experts for help. For a small portion about two and one/half percent, they will work your money for you. And to make your investment grow, cumulate your dividends for you.

The next proposal requires some will power and discipline. It is the fourth principle of money matters. Pay cash for everything you buy, with the exception of your place of habitat. Credit cards and their extreme amounts of interest are suffocating.

Out of your surplus, save a portion for others, the poor, or your charities. What you give will be magnified in return to you. Or you will be blessed in spiritual ways which are beyond your understanding.

Money is not all that matters in life. So the final thing I would like you to know is that purposive acts of kindness will multiply an abundance of love. One of the sensations of the heart when applied to others, the bounty of the world will return to you. Such love is like the boomerang, when if thrown properly, it will return. This is the way of loving kindness. Good deeds bring good thoughts and feelings about life and the world.

Dad

<u>AFTER THOUGHTS</u>

Dear Kids,   October 4, 1997

Re: Unfinished Business

I write this first comment to you–my one and only son. It is not in the form
of a goodbye, "I told you so", or anything of this sort.

A few weeks ago in a heated moment between us, I told you that one
day I would not be around and you may have said something you would later
be sorry for. I want to say to you that anything you ever said in the past was
stated in a moment of passion has been received and forgiven, but to forgive
is not the intent of this note.

If you have any unfinished business with your father, please take care of
it soon for soon, time will be no longer. It appears to me now that I will not
be around nearly as long as I had anticipated or hoped. At least this is the
reading I get from my heart attack.

I don't want you to have to make a trip to my grave and do some
unfinished business. Do it now! Before it's too late. It's later than you think
and it's later than I realize.

The only unfinished business I have with you, Jeff, is to invite you to a
party. The party is life and the host is God. Please come to a life believing
in God and through God it becomes immensely easier than doing it on your
own. Some think it a crutch or copout. I know it's the way of strength and
power.

I hope that you walk with God, Jeff, but if you do, let it be out of your
own conviction and not from the request of a dying father.

I love you dearly, Jeff. I am very proud of you in every way a father can
be proud of his son. I hope if and when you have children, you can remember
me a little bit to them. Take them fishing, play football and baseball with
them. Love them as I forgot at times to love you. Spend time with them.

And honor their mother. Love life dearly and make the very best of it.
Be compassionate and selfless in giving to others. Pray often, read much, and
play hard. May God bless you always?

Dad

Intensive Care Unit
Lethbridge Regional Hospital
October 5, 1997

Dear Jenni,

Re: My first born

As the first born you always carried the heavy stuff in our family. I feel very bad that we experimented in parenting on you. Your shoulders were not big enough to carry that load of us making you into that especially "special" girl. It wasn't until later we discovered you as not special, but our very own daughter whom we loved very much.

Thank God! As I now face the nadir of my life, I also have shed the expectations for you to be someone you could not be because they did not embody you. It's you, Jenni; it's you I really love and not my expectation for you. It's you that I am so proud of and thankful to God for loaning you to us for this brief sojourn on this planet. It's your warmth, humor, and smile I cherish as your father.

The most important thing I am thankful for is your desire and courage to be your own self. It is surely your divine gift to the world. Some things come to us through genetics, such as your manic depressive illness, and I suppose some other things, but to be who you are in life according to who you want to be is your key to success.

I want you to play and to dance in the fields where angels sing. Angel's songs do not have boundaries. Yours, Jen, is a life to enjoy, after you have explored your reasons for being. You make music in your heart, and laughter in the soul. I yearn for you to be happy and contented.

Some of God's children have chosen more difficult paths to walk than others. You, my eldest, have chosen a more difficult path. Somehow the flowers you smell along the way will be beautiful and fragrant beyond your imagination. The rainbows you see will dazzle you with their brilliance.

My daughter, I don't know much about art – but I know you love it. I hope it can be an avocation for you. I hope it can bring you some of the satisfactions of your hearts desire.

I hope you find you, Jenni. To know, accept, and love her as I love you. Always walk with your friend, God, and let yourself leave that peace which you so richly deserve. Happy days! Happy years! Happy eternities!

Your loving dad

Dear Kids,

Re: Life Experiences Can Provide Lessons

There is always some life experience which definitely provide a lesson. Usually these are moments serving as turning points in life. I write you these words at a significant turning point in my life and because of this turning point; I must write this note to each one of you and try to get these letters to press.

Two days ago, I suffered a heart attack. The agony and the pain of it were fairly easy to take, but the hardest part of all, and it is just beginning to settle in now, is that I am not invincible. I am going to die someday and that might not be too far off. Biblically we are given three score and ten, but mine may be sooner as I will just turn 60 in December.

The age of a person means less than how well one has lived their life. Has one seen enough? Done enough? Really lived? Answers must be purely individualistic and meaningful only in the context of one doing the answering.

I can honestly say that my life has contained some gaps – some incomplete sentences and some parts of life not complete. On the other hand, there is little in life that I wanted to accomplish which has not been accomplished except for one wish of mine quite out of my control.

I wish for my children to be the people they choose and want to be, not who I want them to be but who themselves choose to be, in their own right. I realize that time doesn't go on forever and just before the end you will find that time is no longer. Time begins to stand still and then it is no longer. We must learn to be timeless beings.

Please know what you want in life, believe in yourself, and give it all the gusto you can muster. Mostly believe in yourselves, after God that is.

Deep down, I don't believe we choose who our parents are in this world. Nor do I believe we choose our siblings. I do hope long after I'm gone – and your mom too – that you look in on each other and if anyone needs a helping hand you will provide it.

What lasts for eternity is obviously not the physical form. It is the sentimental things we create in life and cherish them to our graves. The touch of your hand, the beauty of your smile, the tenderness behind a birthday gift, the small rift of a disagreement between us, all and more are sweet touches of each something greater. I hope long after I am gone from this earth you will share with each other.

In this round at least, you only go around once. Make the most of it by lifting up your brother or sisters a little bit. Be of good cheer, oh! my children, let my spirit rest in peace by knowing that you love each other, care about each other, and will look out for each other.

Dad

ANOTHER IMPORTANT AFTER THOUGHT

Dear Julie and Jennifer,

Re: Two Budding Teenagers

I write this to the two of you since both of you came as a package many years following our natural born children. I don't remember the year or the day when Social Services asked my wife and me if we would be interested in raising the two of you, but I do remember how quickly we jumped at the chance.

Our biological children were grown and gone from our home. Shari and I realized how vacant our home would be without the sound of familiar voices. We readily assented to have you move in and it wasn't long until the courts assigned us as your legal guardians. The record of your history with us is different from our own kids. Your characters, temperaments and values were all well developed by the time you came to live with us. We did not have the opportunity to mold you as part of our family clay. Thus, you were expected to mix in to an extant unit. We were the clay that needed to be shaped – to meet the needs of two budding teenagers.

So you lived another life before coming to live with us, another with us, and still another as you have moved into your own homes and began raising your own children. The hope for eternal life is that those lessons your parents tried to institute to you and in you had enough imprint for you to pass them along to your kids, while at the same time providing enough know how to help them become individuals in their own.

We are prone to ask and must succumb to the temptation of learning about which we are ourselves. Who am I really? What am I really like? It's only one step aside from this, but somewhere along the line you also ask what you want your own children to be like and do your level best to see that happens according to your desire.

As Shari and I asked this and answered in the same vein about the two of you, we failed to realize that such questions had already been answered for us. You both were fully yourselves when you came to us. All we needed to do was put on the final touches. It didn't always work as we planned, the seeds of two acorns were there to make the mighty oak grow, but we did our level best. It did not always work.

Now as you tend life stepping tip-toe through adulthood; you must make those sacrifices of being parents; you must hear the cries of young heartaches and despair and the glee of a young one chasing a butterfly. It's now up to each of you. God Bless you and good parenting.

Love,

Your only real dad

Acknowledgements

To: All Children Everywhere

I learned much about life from my dad. These memos are some of my own dad's Beliefs. A father and his children enjoy being together. Indeed, they need to be together.

Intimacy is important. From this we learn to express ourselves through our emotions coming from our beliefs. They make up our **lessons on life.** Dad's lessons were so important to me I am passing them on to you hoping they will impact you like they did me.

I am passing on to you bits of his credo which became my very own.

My Dear Grand Children, you will be young when grandpa dies, so your grandpa wants to share part of his Philosophy with you. This is the purpose of these memos.

These musings are a special gift to Jeff (grandson Tyson), Jenni (grandson Calvin), Julie (grandchildren Tessa, Ryan and Levi), and Jennifer (grand children Seth, Katelyn, Cody and Shelby).

All of you have given Grandpa his ultimate meaning in life. My life has trudged through the spiritual death of alcoholism, lived with manic depression for over 40 years, was troubled with diabetes, had a heart attack, and afflicted kidney failure with predictable dialysis in the future. I am working hard to delay it and already I am a year past the predictions. Still life is great, as they say now days **awesome**.

The problems I mention were punctuated with a short lived but successful and contented career as a university teacher. The teaching years left me an strong motivation *of " doing instead of dying"* - to live in the solution rather the problems of death defying obstacles.

These memos would be beneficial to anyone seeking positive beliefs to pass on to their children. Indeed! They would be a cherished legacy. And for anyone anywhere internalizing these beliefs and developing values based on them would say, "Every day, in every way, I am getting better and better." Taken from Emile Coues auto suggestion!

Ron Parton

Testimonies of Jenni and Jeff

I appreciate very much Their comments!

Jenni, "I would like my son, Calvin, to read grandpa's memos." As she says

"My dad has done more with my son than what the average grandfather does. Like everyone he had his faults and some of them I shared with him. He taught a need for A.A. meetings when he thought it was necessary. More than anything else dad taught me self acceptance. I learned the only script for my perfectionism was defeat because no one can be perfect. Dad taught me to accept myself and believe in myself with all my imperfections.

I would like my son, Calvin; to benefit from grandfather's wisdom, especially about financial planning and spiritual guidance. He developed spiritual awareness from over a quarter century in Alcoholics Anonymous and reading virtually every spiritual book he could get his hands on about spiritual living. These beliefs guided him through his life. Indeed, dad's life was a hands on experience!

Dad taught me the value of acceptance and we hope our son will capture these gems of spiritual wisdom and pass them on to others and hopefully some day use them in his own family.

He encouraged me to believe in myself. I was a perfectionist in my growing years.

Spiritual wisdom is the cornerstone for a happy life. Not only did dad have meaning behind these memos, he artfully put them into practice. I have seen them practiced in his life and look forward to these memos giving a permanent record of some of his beliefs for my son and me.

Jeff says -

"Dad, you have shown me many things in my life. You have taught me about faith. You have taught me about drive and determination. You have always known how to motivate me and teach me to strive for the best in life you have always been there with great advice and with worldly wisdom. If I was down you were there to bring me up or to offer me some encouragement. You have always been there as a shoulder to cry on or just for a listening ear. I cherish the relationship that we have had and will continue to have- The meaning of life the deep conversations that we have had about god, the universe, nature and how things work. You have been an inspiration and guide for me along my journey; my spiritual advisor, mentor and friend. I look forward to my son Ty being able to read dad's lessons for future use. Thanks for everything Dad and Grandpa we love you.

Jeff, Julie and Ty Parton

Most people want to change their circumstances to improve their lives, instead of changing themselves to improve their circumstances.

About the Author

Ron grew up in Idaho. After secondary school, he earned a PhD and taught at five universities. He was a successful teacher until addictions disabled him. Memos is based on a wide variety of academic and personal experience. Insights in Memos are his legacy to those he dearly loves.